TIMOTHÉE CHALAMET IS LIFE

A Superfan's Guide to
All Things We Love about
Timothée Chalamet

KATHLEEN PERRICONE
ILLUSTRATED BY BUTCHER BILLY

CONTENTS

Introduction............................ 5
Part One: Call Me Timothée........... 9
    Made in Manhattan............. 11
    Stage and Screen............... 17
    Going Hollywood 23
    "The New Brando".............. 29
    Generational Talent 35
Part Two: Drama King 41
    Filmography 43
Part Three: Chalamania 93
    Timothée A to Z................. 95
Part Four: Hollywood "It" Boy........ 125
    Modern Movie Star 127
    The Internet's Boyfriend 137
    Best Dressed 145
    Everyone's Favorite Costar 151
    Timmy's Top Ten 159
Acknowledgments 167
About the Author 167

INTRODUCTION

No one in Hollywood right now is doing it quite like Timothée Chalamet. An actor whose talent is as distinctive as his quirky personality, he's equally critically acclaimed (thirty-nine awards and counting) and adored by millions of Chalamaniacs. And what's not to love? He can sing and dance, speak three languages, and play the piano and guitar—he even juggles! He's a fashion icon who slays every red carpet he steps foot on, sometimes shirtless beneath a tailored suit made of sustainable fabric. He's a wholesome sex symbol who's just as beautiful on the inside as he is on the outside: creative, emotionally intelligent, amiable, gracious, enthusiastic, a good friend, and a loving son.

Acting since he was a kid, Timothée graduated from commercials and high school productions to television, Broadway, and, ultimately, film. His big-screen debut was in 2014's *Interstellar* directed by Christopher Nolan—whose masterpiece *The Dark Knight* inspired twelve-year-old Timmy to take acting more seriously. A decade later, he got the opportunity to showcase his brilliance by playing a bi-curious teenager in 1980s Italy, in Luca Guadagnino's *Call Me by*

Timothée has won over fans of all generations—and effectively reinvented what it means to be a movie star.

Your Name. A powerful performance, it earned Timothée recognition at the 2018 Academy Awards, where he made history as the youngest Best Actor nominee since nineteen-year-old Mickey Rooney in 1939.

Since his breakthrough, Timothée has built a reputation as one of the most versatile actors with a filmography to prove it. His movies have spanned arthouse flicks and big-budget blockbusters in the genres of drama (*Beautiful Boy*), history (*The King*), science fiction (*Dune* franchise), political satire (*Don't Look Up*), romantic horror (*Bones and All*), and even musical comedy (*Wonka*). We've seen him portray a cannibal and a candy maker; battle drug addiction and tame sandworms; lead medieval England to war and sing about the changing times of post-war America. Timothée's ability to transform into each of these complex characters is what has made him such an in-demand actor.

Simply by being his authentic self, Timothée has won over fans of all generations—and effectively reinvented what it means to be a movie star. It's a winning combination that has added up to generational success at the box office. In 2024, Timothée broke John Travolta's forty-year record of starring in two top-grossing films in the span of eight months with *Wonka* and *Dune: Part Two*, which grossed a combined $1.34 billion. The feat only affirmed the trajectory of his career. "It really just encouraged me to keep using the shades of color or paint that I want to use when I do [act]," Timothée admitted to *GQ*. "All right, let me just continue to trust what I want to work on, big or small."

PART ONE

Call Me Timothée

MADE IN MANHATTAN

The arts are in Timothée Chalamet's DNA: he's the grandson of a Broadway dancer, the son of a musical theater actress, and the brother of a prima ballerina—making him a third-generation performer. His mother, Nicole Flender, who appeared in *Fiddler on the Roof*, *Hello Dolly*, and *A Chorus Line*, had already hung up her dancing shoes by the time Timothée was born on December 27, 1995, but she passed on her love of the performing arts.

Regularly, she took her son and daughter, Pauline, to see plays and musicals around Manhattan, where they lived in a high-rise on 43rd Street just west of the Theater District. "I like to think that the need to act and be seen came from my mom's side," Timothée mused to *GQ*. From his French-born father, Marc Chalamet—a US-based editor for *Le Parisien* newspaper and the United Nations Children's Fund (UNICEF)—he inherited "the ability to listen."

Following in the footsteps of his mother and maternal grandmother, Enid Flender, Timmy got into acting at an early age, mostly in television commercials—work that he didn't find particularly thrilling. "That wasn't acting. It was show business," he confessed to *Verge*. "Because when you are four or five, you're standing in front of the camera, holding up a brand product and smiling as big as you can." His older sister, on the other hand, was passionate about dance, which she studied at the American School of Ballet, their mother's alma mater. Timmy tagged along for her performances at the famed Lincoln Center; however, as a boy he preferred playing in the theater's costume closet over watching the show. "I spent almost the entirety of seven through twelve backstage at Lincoln Center, just running around, waiting for *The Nutcracker* to end," he joked to *Variety* in 2017.

It was after one of Pauline's ballet recitals, in the summer of 2008, that the bored twelve-year-old begged his mother and grandmother to take him to see *The Dark Knight*, the second film in Christopher Nolan's Batman trilogy, starring Christian Bale as the superhero and Heath Ledger as the villainous Joker. "We went to AMC Empire 25 in Times Square for a 7:30 p.m. screening," he reminisced a decade later as the 2018 Best Actor winner at the New York Film Critics Circle Awards. "I left that theater a changed man, and I'm serious about that. Heath Ledger's performance in

> *"I gave him the highest score
> I've ever given a kid auditioning."*

that film was visceral and viral to me, and I now had the acting bug." He scratched the itch, so to speak, with small roles on TV: a murder victim on Season 19 of *Law & Order* and the young version of the male lead in the Hallmark movie *Loving Leah*.

    To become a better actor, Timmy applied to the prestigious Fiorello H. LaGuardia High School of Music & Art and Performing Arts, which boasts famous alumni Jennifer Aniston, Sarah Paulson, Adrien Brody, and Nicki Minaj—also his mother, Nicole, who graduated in 1975. But three decades later, it wouldn't be a simple legacy admission for Timmy "because of poor grades and poor behavior in middle school," he confessed to broadway.com. Harry Shifman, a longtime drama teacher at LaGuardia, was "very incensed" to learn from Pauline, one of his students, that her brother had been rejected. "I remember his audition because I gave him the highest score I've ever given a kid auditioning," Shifman recalled to

Vanity Fair. "He was really that good, and he must have been, I don't know, thirteen at the time. It was riveting. He did two monologues, and then I think we had him read his scene. It was already clear that this kid was so interesting and gifted and compelling." Shifman petitioned the vice principal, who ultimately agreed to admit the young talent. "Thank god she did, because, I don't know, he'd probably be in medical school now." (Actually, he had plans to become a soccer player.)

After finally getting accepted, Timmy's four years at LaGuardia sharpened his natural skills, but more so, deepened his love of acting. For the first time, he saw it as a craft, not the "machine of fakeness" he had witnessed on the sets of TV commercials as a kid. "My first day in high school changed everything," he told *Verge*. "I learned that I had to dive into my work and do research for my parts. I have my teachers to thank for believing in me. They had faith in me. And eventually I started believing in myself."

Shifman, who became Timmy's mentor, taught his protégé an invaluable lesson by *not* casting him in any of the school's productions during his first three years. The competition was tight among the talented student body, with hundreds of hopefuls vying for as little as thirty-five roles. As a sophomore, Timmy auditioned for *Hairspray* yet was passed over for upperclassman and future Hollywood star Ansel Elgort—a rejection that ultimately helped him "come to terms" with his insecurities. "That's the biggest gift you can learn through acting: You are flawed. Everyone is flawed," Timothée explained to *Verge*. "And you can spend your whole life hating yourself because of your flaws—or you can come to accept them and try to make the most of them."

And that he did. The summer before his junior year at LaGuardia, Timmy landed a main role in *The Talls*, an off-Broadway coming-of-age play set in 1970 California. The production received tepid reviews from critics; however, there was a standout in the ensemble cast: "Chalamet hilariously captures a tween's awakening curiosities about sex," praised the *New York Daily News*. With his confidence boosted, he returned to school a completely different actor—and scored the male lead in *Sweet Charity*. In the musical, Timmy's character, Oscar, is memorably introduced when Charity, a lovelorn dancer, gets stuck in an elevator with the claustrophobic tax accountant. On opening night at LaGuardia's concert hall, the sixteen-year-old had the audience in stitches as he acted out Oscar's overdramatic panic, punctuated by the musical number "I'm the Bravest Individual." Shifman, who directed the play, was the most impressed. "In my entire life, and I'm in my mid-sixties, I have never seen a more brilliant comic performance [than] Timmy gave in that scene," he gushed years later to *Vanity Fair*, as his former student's breakthrough in *Call Me by Your Name* earned him a 2018 Academy Award nomination for Best Actor. "Anybody who saw it would say so."

STAGE AND SCREEN

While still in high school, Timothée put himself on a tight deadline for success. "I had a delusional dream in my early teenage years to have, in my late teenage years, an acting career," he recalled to British *Vogue* in 2022. At the age of sixteen, he landed a four-episode arc on USA's *Royal Pains*, and even more high-profile, the role of Vice President Walden's son Finn on Showtime's Emmy Award–winning series *Homeland*, in 2012. By then, "I felt like I reduced my goal to something more realistic, which was to work in theater and hopefully make enough money doing either a TV show or something I could sustain myself [with]. And then it felt like every dream came true, exponentially."

"I've always felt like there was less creative space on sets with guardians."

As his senior year of high school came to a close, Timothée's agent, his mother, and even *Homeland* costar Claire Danes convinced him not to rush out to Hollywood just yet. In 2013, he enrolled at Columbia University, an Ivy League institution in Manhattan, to study cultural anthropology—but acting remained his main focus. That summer, Timothée traveled to Canada to film Christopher Nolan's space drama *Interstellar*, but the seventeen-year-old didn't want his parents to come along, so he found a loophole in the law: "For films made by production companies based out of the West Coast, if you have a high school degree and are over sixteen then you can travel alone," he recalled to the *Los Angeles Times*. "I just told my parents I was going alone. I've always felt like there was less creative space on sets with guardians. I just felt independent at a young age."

The experience on *Interstellar* was life-altering for Timothée. Not only was he working with the director of one of his favorite movies, *The Dark Knight*, but he also forged a deep bond with his onscreen father played by Matthew McConaughey. Resuming life back in New York as a college student, "I just kind of floundered," he later admitted to McConaughey in a conversation for *Interview* magazine. "Columbia takes a wholehearted academic commitment that I think I have in me, but it was just not where my mind was at the time. I'd just left working a month and a half in Canada with my favorite director and you, one of my favorite actors, and had to go back into a structured environment. It was just hard."

There was more distraction in the spring semester when Timothée took time away from school to film Jason Reitman's *Men, Women & Children* with an ensemble cast featuring Jennifer Garner, Adam Sandler, and his LaGuardia classmate Ansel Elgort. He struggled to find a balance between school and work, and in anticipation of his two films arriving in theaters that fall, Timothée dropped out of Columbia ahead of his sophomore year. It was a decision he would soon come to regret. Most of his scenes in *Men, Women & Children* ended up on the cutting room floor, yet he still went to the premiere (and sulked at the after-party). Weeks later, when *Interstellar* was released in November 2014, Timothée confessed to *Time*, "I remember seeing it and weeping. Sixty percent because I was so moved by it, and forty percent because I'd thought I was in the movie so much more than I am."

His next film was a costarring role with *Mad Men*'s Kiernan Shipka in *One & Two*, about a brother and sister who live in isolation with their religious family—and possess the power of teleportation. The 2015 indie flick was not well-received by critics, who seemed to barely notice Timothée (aside from *Variety* pointing out he "unconvincingly" handled a pitchfork in a farming scene). In another role playing the younger version of James Franco's character in *The Adderall Diaries*, he was lost in the film's negative reviews. Critics were even harsher on the Christmas comedy *Love the Coopers*, although the young actor got to share the screen with veterans Diane Keaton and John Goodman.

It was a seasoned pro of the stage, Tony Award–winning playwright John Patrick Shanley, who changed everything when he cast Timothée as his younger, misfit self in the autobiographical play *Prodigal Son*. The twenty-year-old wanted the role so badly, he auditioned three times before being personally selected by Shanley, whose Pulitzer Prize–winning drama, *Doubt: A Parable*, was adapted for a 2008 film starring Meryl Streep, Phillip Seymour Hoffman, Amy Adams, and Viola Davis—all of whom earned Academy Award nominations for their performances. A complicated character "on the verge of salvation or destruction," *Prodigal Son* required an equally complex actor. "What I needed was somebody who you would believe could write a poem—and would hit you," Shanley explained to broadway.com. "I could find guys who [looked like they] could write a poem or hit you; to find both was harder. I saw some talented young men, but Timothée had that unquantifiable extra element you need to create magic. I thought, 'I need to hire this guy.'"

Shanley's opinion was validated by composer Paul Simon moments into the first dress rehearsal. "'Kid's good,' he whispered," Shanley recalled to *Vulture*. "Then he watched a little more and said, 'Kid's very good.' That, to Paul, is like gigantic shouting." And he wasn't the only voice. When *Prodigal Son* premiered off-Broadway at the Manhattan Theatre Club in February 2016, critics raved over the relative unknown's stage debut. *The Hollywood Reporter* heralded Timothée as "a real discovery," while the

New York Times predicted that the "gifted" actor was destined for greatness: "He fills a tall order of a character with enough easy charisma to confirm his status as a rising star." That year, Timothée won the Lucille Lortel Award for Outstanding Lead Actor in a Play—beating out four-time Oscar nominee Ed Harris—and earned a Drama League Award nomination for Distinguished Performance, losing to *Hamilton*'s Lin-Manuel Miranda.

Days after *Prodigal Son* ended its six-week run, Timothée hopped on a flight to Italy for his next project as the starring role in an adaptation of the coming-of-age novel *Call Me by Your Name*. It was three years earlier when he met with director Luca Guadagnino, a lucky break made possible by his agent Brian Swardstrom, whose husband was producing the film. Guadagnino cast Timothée on the spot, yet it would be some time before he could raise the necessary capital. "It looked like perhaps it was going to come together that summer . . . and it didn't," Timothée recalled to *Rolling Stone*. "And then maybe the following summer . . . and it didn't." But there was something about the story that convinced him to wait it out. "It was complex, layered, contradictory, real, and relatable—it was an awesome and accurate lens into what a young person experiences." *Call Me by Your Name* ended up being Timmy's breakout role, officially inserting himself as a talent of the Hollywood film industry.

GOING HOLLYWOOD

Timothée knew *Call Me by Your Name*, a coming-of-age film about queer romance, would make or break his career—but to what degree? "It always seemed to me that the worst-case scenario was I'd be walking the street five years from now and somebody might come up to me and say, 'Hey, you had sex with a peach in that movie once,'" he joked to the *Los Angeles Times*. But when that movie premiered at the Sundance Film Festival in January 2017, all critics could talk about was the newcomer's "breathtaking," "stunning," and "transfixing" performance.

The buzz grew louder over the following months ahead of *Call Me by Your Name*'s release. Timothée prepared himself for the press tour by watching early interviews of Academy Award–winning actress Jennifer Lawrence and NBA superstar Lebron James, studying how they handled themselves. He was featured in the pages of *Vogue*, interviewed on *Jimmy Kimmel Live!*, and even graced the cover of *GQ Style* next to the proclamation "A Star Is Born." As the discussion moved to his Academy Award-worthy performance, the magazine asked Timothée if at the age of twenty-one, it was too soon. "Look, I went for a huge film two years ago that I didn't get, and I was devastated for about six months," he admitted. "So I'm pinching myself now, that aside from academic evaluations of the film, having seen people viscerally react to it at Sundance and Berlin . . . what it's already been has been more than I could've ever asked for."

Call Me by Your Name was just one of Timothée's three acclaimed films that year. At the 2017 Telluride Film Festival, critics also got their first look at his other two projects: Greta Gerwig's directorial debut, *Lady Bird*, and the Western drama *Hostiles* starring Christian Bale. Timothée had auditioned for the latter film via video while making *Call Me by Your Name* in Italy, and he headed straight to its New Mexico set to play a young cavalry soldier who must escort a dying Native American war chief back to his home in Montana. After wrapping *Hostiles*, he was off to Los Angeles to film his scenes in *Lady Bird* as the lead character's unlikable love interest. It was a small role that made a big impact on moviegoers and especially the director. Gerwig, who first saw Timothée onstage in *Prodigal Son*, described him to *GQ* as "a heartthrob but with thoroughbred acting chops. Everyone else will be amazed by what he grows into, but I won't—I've always known that he's a unicorn."

*"I've always known
that he's a unicorn."*

It didn't take long for the rest of the world to see the same. That award season, Timothée was honored everywhere from the US (Los Angeles Film Critics Association, Chicago Film Critics Association, Gotham Independent Film Awards) to the UK (London Film Critics Circle). The major associations all recognized his work with nominations for *Call Me by Your Name*: Golden Globe Awards, Screen Actors Guild Awards, Critics Choice Awards—and the highest merit, the Academy Awards in 2018. He was up for Best Actor alongside Daniel Day-Lewis (*Phantom Thread*), Daniel Kaluuya (*Get Out*), Denzel Washington (*Roman J. Israel, Esq.*), and Gary Oldman, who won for his portrayal of Winston Churchill in *Darkest Hour*. On the biggest night of his career thus far, Timothée brought along his mother Nicole, who nurtured his love of acting from a young age. She was beaming with pride next to her talented son on the red carpet. But as

Timothée joked to *Vulture*, she was just happy that people might finally spell his name correctly. "On the projects I was working on when I was twelve, thirteen, fourteen, she was sending many an email to non-obliging producers saying, 'It's not Timothy with a y, there's an accent on the first 'e,' and the accent faces this way!'"

Timothée's name seemed to be everywhere as the promising star skyrocketed to internet fame as well. "His haircuts are breaking news stories," reported *Time Out London*. Out in the real world, he was recognized everywhere. In line at Chipotle, a fan dropped a bag of peach candies on the counter in front of him and ran off. (He ate them, but only after ensuring the seal wasn't broken.) In Hungary, while filming Netflix's medieval epic *The King*, "a Mercedes screeched up next to me. I thought: What's going on here? Then a little girl jumped out and had a *Call Me by Your Name* phone case and wanted me to sign these things."

The famous actor got to be a fanboy, too. He shared the screen with Steve Carell—the star of his favorite television show, *The Office*—in 2018's *Beautiful Boy*. Based on the true story of a father's fight to save his son from addiction, the film had a powerful impact—especially for its lead actor, who was truly transformed by the experience. On a personal level, the movie was "my get," Timothée revealed to Emma Stone in *Variety*'s Actors on Actors video series. "Everything else I weirdly kind of stumbled into, including *Call Me by Your Name* and *Lady Bird*. [*Beautiful Boy*] was the thing where I went into the LA audition room and did it again and again and again." When he got the part, *then* came "an added pressure." Timothée threw himself so deeply into the role of down-and-out addict Nic Sheff, it remains one of his most spell-binding performances yet.

RARE REJECTIONS

During the years Timothée struggled to land his breakout role, he was *this close* several times. In 2015, he auditioned for *Manchester by the Sea*, a part opposite Casey Affleck as a teenage boy whose life is turned upside down by the sudden death of his father. Not only did it go to Lucas Hedges, who earned an Academy Award nomination for his performance, but *Manchester by the Sea* is also considered one of the best films of the twenty-first century. The following year, he was also passed over for the reboot of *Spider-Man*, a Marvel Cinematic Universe franchise that made Tom Holland a household name. (Ironically, he went on to beat out Holland for the lead in 2023's *Wonka*.) Timothée had read twice for the superhero role, but both attempts were disastrous. "I left sweating in a total panic," he recalled at the 2018 Los Angeles Film Critics Association Awards. His anxiety peaked when he tried out for *White Boy Rick*, a crime drama about the youngest FBI informant. "I wept for hours after doing that audition," Timothée confessed to *Time Out* in October 2018, after the film languished in theaters.

"THE NEW BRANDO"

Timothée has most notably been compared to Marlon Brando, but with each acclaimed performance, the list grows longer. In his review of *Beautiful Boy*, Richard Roeper reasoned, "To me his work is more reminiscent of James Dean—electric and forceful and screen-grabbing, but stunningly vulnerable and real." *Lady Bird* director Greta Gerwig, who cast Timothée in 2019's *Little Women*, was reminded of contemporaries: "a young Christian Bale crossed with a young Daniel Day-Lewis with a sprinkle of young Leonardo DiCaprio." *The Hollywood Reporter*'s Sherri Linden argued that the Louisa May Alcott adaptation proved Timothée as an inheritor of Montgomery Clift's "elegant transmutation of emotional complexity, unpredictability, and physical nuance."

"I'm really still learning and trying to chase whatever best version of an actor I can be."

In his 2018 conversation with Emma Stone for *Variety*, Timothée described his career thus far as a novel with 2016's *Miss Stevens*, about a teen who discovers his true self in drama class, as the "prelude," followed by Chapter One: *Call Me by Your Name* and Chapter Two: *Beautiful Boy*. In 2019, there were two strong contenders for Chapter Three, *The King* and *Little Women*. Both period pieces, albeit set four centuries apart, demanded a different facet of the young actor's artistry. "I'm really trying to just do great projects and things that are challenging," he told the Associated Press. "I feel I'm really still learning and trying to chase whatever best version of an actor I can be."

The King, based on Shakespeare's *Henriad*, is the story of Henry V of England, who reluctantly inherits the throne—and a war started by his malevolent father—following Henry IV's death in 1413. The epic medieval film was the biggest movie budget Timothée had ever worked on to date, his first to require stunt work, and so far, the only to yield a workplace romance. (He reportedly dated his onscreen wife, Lily-Rose Depp, for over a year.) To portray a warrior-king, Timothée spent six weeks learning how to sword fight and ride a horse while wearing a bulky suit of armor. These were fantasy scenarios that originally made him "want to become an actor," he told *Vanity Fair*. "It sounds absurd to say out loud. Even so, that was exhilarating."

There were some harsh realities on the set of *The King*, like the film's climax scene of the famed Battle of Agincourt between England and France (led by Robert Pattinson's Dauphin). One sequence required Timothée to charge into battle on foot, across a dense muddy field no less, four times in a row to get the perfect shot. But he knew what he was signing up for: when Timothée first read the script, he thought, "I'm sure whoever does this is gonna have a great time doing it," he joked to BBC Radio 1. He read it a second time, and still struggled to see himself pulling off most of the scenes—which is ultimately why he decided to take it on. "There are roles that terrify you and I think those are good to do sometimes." Plus, he got to take home a pretty sweet souvenir from the set: King Henry V's metal helmet.

As mature and poised as Timothée was for his age—twenty-three when *The King* premiered on Netflix in November 2019—there were still some obvious signs of his youth. During promotion for the film in New York, *Vanity Fair* witnessed an exchange between the millennial actor and director David Michôd. In the middle of a conversation, Timothée "reflexively" pulled out his cell phone to read a text message and was "swiftly reprimanded by Michôd, who cleared his throat and motioned with his fingers to make eye contact."

Timothée went from a king to a princely lord in *Little Women*, his second time working with director Greta Gerwig and costar Saoirse Ronan from *Lady Bird*. In a supporting role as Laurie, the charming dandy who lives next door to the March sisters, he was a novelty among the female cast of Florence Pugh, Emma Watson, Laura Dern, and Meryl Streep. In Louisa May Alcott's 1868 book, Laurie is friend-zoned by Jo (Ronan), a complicated relationship that peaks when she turns down his marriage proposal. It's a significant scene that has driven the countless film adaptations, but in 2019, Timothée revitalized the moment, begging Jo to reconsider with a "swoony, panicky heartache for the ages," praised *The Hollywood Reporter*. "I love that in *Lady Bird*, you broke my heart," Ronan joked to Timothée in a joint interview with *Entertainment Weekly*. "In *Little Women*, I got to break your heart."

The two actors, arguably the most talented of their Hollywood generation, credited their offscreen friendship for the chemistry between Jo and Laurie. After wrapping *Little Women*, Timothée reunited with Ronan a third time for *The French Dispatch*, Wes Anderson's quirky comedic drama about American journalists stationed at a news bureau in Paris. With an ensemble cast including Owen Wilson, Tilda Swinton, Bill Murray, and Frances McDormand, Timmy and Saoirse unfortunately didn't get to share the screen—and he's barely on it for twenty minutes himself. However, Anderson did write the character of Zeffirelli, a student revolutionary, specifically for Timothée. "I never had the inconvenience of ever thinking of anybody else for this role even for a second," the director told *GQ*. "I knew he was exactly right."

Timothée and Ronan nearly had a fourth film collaboration as cameos in Gerwig's highly anticipated live-action *Barbie* as rejected dolls, but their busy schedules didn't allow it. (He was in England shooting *Wonka*.) Chalamaniacs were also robbed of another promising performance in what could've been Timothée's London stage debut in *4000 Miles*, a play that explores grief and family through late-night conversations between a young man and his widowed grandmother. Set to open in April 2020, the production was fully rehearsed when the COVID-19 pandemic forced its postponement just weeks before the curtain rose at the Old Vic Theatre. When the American actor's casting was first announced, ticket sales for *4000 Miles* hit record-setting numbers. British *Vogue* reported, "The news was met with a level of hysteria not usually associated with the 202-year-old theatre's crowd." Two years later, when it was ultimately canceled due to rescheduling conflicts, fan reactions were just as intense. "To say I'm absolutely gutted is an understatement," wrote one ticket holder on Twitter (now known as X). "I'll never see Timothée Chalamet up close," lamented another. But never say never: Timothée believes he will one day return to the stage.

GENERATIONAL TALENT

Still in his twenties, Timothée is in a class all his own in Hollywood. There are only a few millennial actors who even come close to his level of dramatic talent, save Tom Holland, arguably his greatest competition for coveted roles (and his good friend). Timothée is so elite, he hasn't auditioned for anything since 2016—the year before *Call Me by Your Name*—which his agent Brian Swardstrom revealed in a viral 2023 tweet to refute rumors that the Academy Award nominee was contending with Paul Mescal, Austin Butler, and Miles Teller for the lead in Ridley Scott's *Gladiator II*.

But that doesn't mean Timothée doesn't fight for the films he wants. Back in 2013, the seventeen-year-old auditioned for Denis Villeneuve's *Prisoners*, a thriller starring Hugh Jackman and Jake Gyllenhaal, but didn't get the part. Determined to work with the French filmmaker, years later when he learned Villeneuve was directing the sci-fi epic *Dune*, he set up a Google alert on his phone to keep track of the latest developments and started reading Frank Herbert's 1965 novel about the fight for the desert planet Arrakis. Timothée and Villeneuve both attended the 2017 *Deadline Contenders* event, where the latter was promoting *Blade Runner 2049*, and Timothée later told *Deadline*, "I remember I was trying to put myself in front of him as much as possible and set up a meeting with him." At the 2018 British Academy Film Awards, Timothée spotted Villeneuve across the room and went over to talk to him, but "didn't really get a sense of the possibility [of working with him]."

Six months later, Timothée was about halfway through Herbert's six-hundred-page book when he got the call he had been waiting for: Villeneuve wanted to meet to discuss playing Paul Atreides, the lead in *Dune*. "I quickly busted through the second half of the book as best I could," Timothée told *Deadline*. "So, like, the first half of my copy is properly annotated and full of my thoughts, and then the second half I just raced through. And then I had that meeting with him, and it was such a joy." The pleasure was all Villeneuve's. He later admitted in an interview with SiriusXM, "I was the one stalking him. Let's say the truth is I was dreaming to add Timothée on board."

Dune, which also stars Zendaya, grossed $407.6 million worldwide in 2021—and a sequel was immediately given the green light by Warner Bros. When Timothée returned for *Part Two*, Villeneuve saw a very

> *"It was the first time that I witnessed someone growing in front of my camera."*

different actor, one who had been transformed by his first leading role in a major-studio production. "In *Part One*, the camera was capturing the performance of a teenager—I'm talking about the character, someone who was learning about the world and experiencing a new reality," the director told *GQ*. "But *Part Two* is really about someone who goes from the boy to the man, and becomes a leader, and even, I will say, a dark charismatic, messianic figure. It was the first time that I witnessed someone growing in front of my camera." *Dune: Part Two* arrived in theaters in 2024, and nearly doubled its predecessor's box-office numbers—prompting discussion of a possible third *Dune* film.

In between *Dune*'s two installments, Timothée starred in another pair of films that explored new cinematic genres: the romantic-horror film *Bones and All* and the musical comedy *Wonka*. The first project reunited the actor with Luca Guadagnino, the director who changed his life with *Call Me by Your Name* just three years earlier. Months into the 2020 pandemic, Guadagnino sent him a script unlike anything ever written before, a cannibal love story that's as romantic as it is grotesque. Timothée not only agreed to star in *Bones and All*, but he also signed on as a producer and leveraged his newfound power in Hollywood to secure the necessary funding for the indie production. It was quite the opposite experience on *Wonka*, a big-budget spectacle about the candy man in the years before he opened his world-famous chocolate factory. Directed by *Paddington*'s Paul King, the whimsical prequel includes choreographed musical numbers, Hugh Grant as an Oompa Loompa (with the help of CGI, of course), and a magical world of pure imagination.

Wonka, which pulled in $632 million worldwide, "was a tonal adjustment because the movies I've been in—even something like *Dune* that's eight thousand years in the future—they have a very naturalistic quality, and this was very much old-school storytelling, sort of golden age of musical," Timothée told Rotten Tomatoes. "So, that was a shift and sort of like a stamina adjustment to always be 'on,' because the character—as opposed to the Tim Burton version and the Gene Wilder version—is propelling his own story here. So, it was a new challenge."

All throughout the productions of *Dune*, *Bones and All*, and *Wonka*, Timothée was simultaneously preparing for the role of a lifetime: Bob Dylan in James Mangold's *A Complete Unknown*. Set in the 1960s, during the folk singer's rise to fame, the biographical film focuses on Dylan's controversial decision to pick up an electric guitar at the height of his popularity. The parallels between Timothée and Dylan's lives, six decades apart, was apparent to the young actor. "Bob is like my *Fame for Dummies*," he told *GQ*. "It's a different thing now because there were so few people who were that well-known then that you could really just dodge *everything* and be unknown."

A Complete Unknown arrived in theaters on Christmas Day in 2024, two days before Timothée's twenty-ninth birthday. As he enters his next decade of life—and era of his promising career—his ambitions remain the same as when we first met him in *Call Me by Your Name*. "I want to make movies that matter and speak to people," Timothée revealed to the *South China Morning Post*. "I think it's the role of the artist to shine a light on what's going on."

PART TWO

Drama King

FILMOGRAPHY

A decade's worth of films in his repertoire, Timothée's work spans practically every genre: coming of age, sci-fi, fantasy, comedy, horror, Western—and lots and lots of drama (biographical, historical, romantic). Whether it's a big-budget production (*Dune*, *Wonka*) or smaller arthouse flick, fans know he'll give his all to a role, as proven by the superstar's hundred-plus awards and nominations. "This is an actor whose every performance feels shaped by a deep emotional intelligence," notes *The Hollywood Reporter* film critic Jon Frosch.

CALL ME BY YOUR NAME

TIMOTHÉE CHALAMET COMES OF AGE IN HOLLYWOOD
RELEASE DATE: JANUARY 19, 2018

Seventeen-year-old Elio (Chalamet) falls for an older American man (Armie Hammer) who comes to Italy one summer to work under his father (Michael Stuhlbarg), an esteemed professor of archaeology.

DIRECTOR: Luca Guadagnino

CAST: Armie Hammer, Michael Stuhlbarg

GENRE: Coming-of-age romantic drama

RATED: R

BOX OFFICE: $43.1 million

AWARDS: Academy Awards: Best Actor (nomination); Golden Globes: Best Actor (nomination)

FIRST CHOICE: Timothée was the one and only actor in consideration to portray Elio Perlman, a teenager whose lazy summer in Italy is interrupted by the arrival of a handsome American scholar named Oliver. His indifference toward the visitor develops into a mutual sexual desire that ultimately ends in heartbreak. Timothée had read André Aciman's

2007 novel, *Call Me by Your Name*—"a window into a young person," he told *Variety*—and when he heard about its adaptation, he expressed interest to his manager, Brian Swardstrom, whose husband, Peter Spears, was producing the film. Spears set up a test reading for Timothée with director Luca Guadagnino—and an official audition afterward was no longer necessary. "I felt immediately that he had the ambition, the intelligence, the sensitivity, the naivety, and the artistry to be Elio," Guadagnino recalled to *Screen Prism*.

As for the role of Oliver, Shia LaBeouf had been cast in an early incarnation of the film. But when Guadagnino signed on, he sought out Armie Hammer who had impressed him in *The Social Network*. Timothée didn't meet his onscreen love interest until he arrived on the set in Crema, Italy, and in between rehearsing, the two worked to build their chemistry, spending every moment together for weeks. "Armie and I really hit it off," he told *Variety*. "We became such good friends that it made the chemistry on-screen palpable, because we really did like each other in real life."

GETTING INTO CHARACTER: Timothée wasn't all that different from Elio, a virtuoso of piano and guitar who is fluent in Italian, French, and English—the actor had played both instruments for years and could speak French from his summers visiting his grandparents in Le Chambon-sur-Lignon. To sharpen his tools, he arrived on set five weeks ahead of production for daily lessons: three hours with composer Roberto Solci plus another ninety minutes studying Italian, which was "crucial for me because it was a native tongue for Elio," Timothée said in the film's press kit. He became so skilled at piano and guitar, the soundtrack includes his performance of Bach's "Capriccio on the Departure of his Beloved Brother."

MAKING A SCENE: In the book, the moment Elio confesses his feelings to Oliver is "so genuine," Timothée worried that it might not translate to film. "I felt like that one scene would be a barometer for whether we would pull it off or not," he admitted in *i-D* magazine. Until the day cameras rolled, Guadagnino didn't know how he would shoot the scene, and it was actually Hammer who suggested a wide angle—done in one take, no less. "The unconventional method is what ultimately made the moment," added Timothée. "It took away the whole cringey Hollywood feeling. If you mute the movie, you can't tell it's somebody telling somebody else that they are in love with them."

ROLE REVERSAL: Among the endless accolades for *Call Me by Your Name*, there was also plenty of criticism for romanticizing a sexual relationship between a teenager and an adult. "What I always say to that is . . . it's so clear in watching it how consensual the story is," he explained to the *Toronto Star*. "It's full of love and care. And, in many ways, with Elio being from the town [in the movie] he's in his comfort zone, as opposed to the foreigner, Oliver. Elio is the driver of this relationship in many ways."

UNHAPPY ENDING: The film's "emotional narrator" is its soundtrack, which features three original pieces by American singer-songwriter Sufjan Stevens. Days before the start of production, he submitted the tracks to Guadagnino, who then used them to inspire his actors in specific scenes. For the final sequence—a four-minute static shot of Elio's face as he reels from Oliver's engagement news—Timothée listened to "Visuals of Gideon" via an earpiece "so I could mirror the structure" while tearfully gazing into a crackling fireplace. "It was [a] bit of an acting experiment,"

Chalamet explained in the film's DVD commentary. "I was grateful I had enough personal experiences to draw from. I don't wanna do that all the time . . . [but] with the camera this close and the take being as long as it is—it felt like anything else would ring false."

LITERARY LIBERTIES: The film adaptation differs slightly from Aciman's novel and mostly for cinematic effect. Originally, the novel was set in 1987 and told in flashbacks by Elio. But in the film, Guadagnino nixed the retrospective storytelling "because in a way, it kills the surprise," he explained to *Screen Prism*. His plot plays out over the summer of 1983, several years before the AIDS crisis, so it "could be a little more utopic," Timothée revealed in *VMan* magazine. Guadagnino drew from his own experiences as a gay teen in 1980s Italy for the viral scene in which Elio and Oliver dance in a bar to "Love My Way" by the Psychedelic Furs, one of his favorite songs at the time. He also reworked Aciman's ending: Instead of Elio and Oliver connecting twenty years later, the film concludes in 1983. The author admitted in *Vanity Fair* that "my heart sank" when he first learned of the change. But once he saw the final scene, "I was stunned. The ending captured the very spirit of the novel I had written in ways that I could never have imagined or anticipated."

NEXT CHAPTER: Ever since the film's release, Guadagnino has teased the cinematic continuation of Elio and Oliver's story. The director imagined an additional five-part series starring Chalamet and Hammer, with the first sequel set in 1990 when the younger of the pair would be twenty-five. "How great would it be to see those actors grow older, embodying those characters?" he mused to *Vulture* in 2017. Two years later, Aciman released

the literary sequel, *Find Me*, which follows Elio, his father, Sami, and Oliver over four distinct periods—ending two decades later, with Elio and Oliver together and raising Elio's much younger half-brother after Sami's death.

Just as Guadagnino began preproduction, everything was halted due to the COVID-19 pandemic. When Hollywood resumed filmmaking in 2021, Chalamet's schedule was already filled, between the two-part *Dune* and *Wonka* prequel. As he and Guadagnino focused on other projects, the *Call Me by Your Name* series faded, but only for the foreseeable future. "The truth of the matter is," the director told *Deadline*, "my heart is still there."

BEAUTIFUL BOY

A SOBERING JOURNEY OF ADDICTION AND RECOVERY
RELEASE DATE: SEPTEMBER 30, 2018

In this true story, *New York Times* writer David Sheff (Steve Carell) agonizes over how to save his son Nic (Timothée) from the throes of drug addiction.

DIRECTOR: Felix van Groeningen

CAST: Steve Carell, Maura Tierney, Amy Ryan

GENRE: Biographical drama

RATED: R

BOX OFFICE: $16.6 million

AWARDS: Hollywood Film Awards: Hollywood Supporting Actor; Golden Globes: Best Supporting Actor (nomination); Screen Actors Guild: Outstanding Performance by a Male Actor in a Supporting Role (nomination)

BETTING ON THE BOYS: During the decade *Beautiful Boy* was stuck in preproduction, several young actors were considered for the role of Nic Sheff, whose decade-long battle with drugs (pills, crystal meth, heroin) began when he was a teenager and spiraled into homelessness, two overdoses, multiple rehab stints, and thirteen attempts to finally get clean in his late twenties. In January 2017, when Carell signed on to play Nic's father, David, *The Maze Runner*'s Will Poulter was reportedly set to star opposite *The Office* star. However, in the following month, *The Hollywood Reporter* announced that little-known Timothée had been cast in the role, on the heels of *Call Me by Your Name*'s acclaim at the Sundance Film Festival.

Timmy was handpicked by director Felix van Groeningen, who sifted through two hundred audition tapes to find his Nic—Timmy, who went on to become one of the most popular (and promising) young Hollywood stars by the time *Beautiful Boy* arrived in theaters twenty months later. "There is less burden, now of course, it's great," van Groeningen told Dutch outlet *De Morgen* (Dutch for *The Morning*). "Nobody had foreseen that he would suddenly become world-famous, but it is completely deserved. If [his fame] can help bring young people to the cinema, I can only applaud it."

UNDER THE INFLUENCE: Timothée, twenty-one, had no experience with hard drugs, but he wanted to fully understand the highs and lows—without ingesting any illegal substances, of course. "I did a lot of research and read about drugs, and I brought the books to my first meeting with the director. I could see in his eyes that he was thinking, *This kid is nuts*," Timothée, who also spent time at in-patient facilities, recalled to *W Magazine*. "But I felt this movie—the subject of drug addiction—was so important. I wanted to make an anti-glorification-of-drugs movie. And I think we did."

GOING METHOD: Timothée dropped eighteen pounds (8 kg) from his already-slight frame to accurately portray a drug addict. But as his character falls in and out of sobriety over the course of the film, the first scenes they shot were when Nic was at his unhealthiest, particularly his overdose and hospitalization. The actor then got a week off so he could regain the weight and "look like a healthy Nic," he told *W*. "I went to get spaghetti like that first night, and I was like, 'This is not happening!' I couldn't get it down."

OUT OF CHARACTER: Filming lasted fewer than two months, but the role of Nic stayed with Timothée long after the cameras cut. Going into the project, he was nervous that due to his inexperience as an actor he might lean too far into the seriousness of the role "thinking that was what it would take to make it good," he confessed to Harry Styles in a conversation for *i-D* magazine. Sure enough, the final day of production, "I had the strangest walk home. I didn't even live it, Nic and David did, but I still felt really affected, drained and a little devastated. The movie isn't a downer, because it is really redemptive and hopeful, but it did feel like a punch to the stomach."

HIS STORIES: The biographical drama is told through the perspectives of both father and son, who documented their individual experiences in their respective 2008 memoirs, *Beautiful Boy: A Father's Journey Through His Son's Addiction* and *Tweak: Growing Up on Methamphetamines*. David first shared his story in a 2005 *New York Times Magazine* article, "My Addicted Son," detailing Nic's struggles and the agony to get him clean. *Beautiful Boy* went on to reach No. 1 on the *New York Times* Best Sellers and Amazon ranked it as one of the Best Books of 2008. *Tweak*—also a *New York Times* chart-topper—chronicles Nic's long road to recovery, which he explored further in the 2011 follow-up, *We All Fall Down: Living with Addiction*. Together, the Sheffs wrote 2019's *High: Everything You Want to Know About Drugs, Alcohol, and Addiction*, as a resource for teens.

REAL FRIENDS: To fully understand the character and his experience as a drug addict, Timothée met with the real-life Nic Sheff a week before the start of filming. Timmy was full of "nerves and anxiety," which he admitted to *Variety*, but was "immediately settled by [the] extraordinarily warm and kind and intelligent and wise person that Nic is; that is innate to him but also through his experiences and his life." The two, who are more than a decade apart in age, formed a bond so authentic, they reunited ahead of *Beautiful Boy*'s release to talk addiction awareness at film screenings in Austin and Dallas, Texas; St. Louis, Missouri; and Minneapolis, Minnesota.

For Nic particularly, the film was "an amazing gift," he revealed on the *Today* show in 2018. Now sober and married (and as of 2024, a father), "Watching the movie was such an incredible reminder of everything we went through as a family and how lucky I am to be alive, and how lucky I am to be sitting here with my dad. I came away from it feeling so grateful."

FOR A GOOD CAUSE: The story of *Beautiful Boy* is specific to the Sheff Family, but addiction affects just about everyone. According to a 2023 report by the US Department of Health and Human Services, 61.2 million people aged twelve and over (nearly a quarter of the population) used illicit drugs in the past year. And to Timothée, it was important to show audiences that "addiction doesn't have a face, it has no preferred class, or gender, or race," he told *W*. "I think it's almost easier or something to be like, 'Oh, well, that doesn't affect me or my family or my friends. That's another thing.' When the reality is, it's everywhere. And it's one of my favorite things about the movie, too. And I think it's sometimes uncomfortable for audiences where they go, 'Why?' [The why is] not the point. It just is."

THE KING
COMING FOR THE HOLLYWOOD THRONE
RELEASE DATE: NOVEMBER 1, 2019

When his father dies, Henry V (Timothée) reluctantly becomes England's new monarch and must lead his country to war with France.

DIRECTOR: David Michôd

CAST: Joel Edgerton, Sean Harris, Lily-Rose Depp, Robert Pattinson, Ben Mendelsohn

GENRE: Epic historical drama

RATED: R

BOX OFFICE: $126,931 (limited three-week theatrical release)

AWARDS: The Australian Academy of Cinema and Television Arts Awards: Best Actor in a Leading Role (nomination)

COMPLEX CHARACTER: After *Call Me by Your Name*, *Lady Bird*, and *Beautiful Boy*, Timothée wanted his next role to be the most unexpected. He was particularly eager to work with Australian director David Michôd, whose films tend to shine a light on toxic masculinity, notably the 2010 crime drama *Animal Kingdom*. And with Henry V, Timothée recognized there was a much deeper story to be told about the greatest warrior-king of medieval England. "There's something particular about this movie that I'm proud of which is that it's about . . . someone with good intent—or at least acting with good intent and honor—thrust into a circumstance that, even with decisive action to go in the opposite direction of his father, is weak in comparison to the preexisting institutions of power," the actor explained to *Entertainment Weekly*. "That has contemporary allegories what with leaders we have today who should have no business leading countries."

HISTORICAL FICTION: *The King*, written by Michôd and Edgerton, is based on Shakespeare's *Henriad*, a collection of plays dramatizing the rise of Henry IV and Henry V. The filmmakers took some liberties of their own, adding in historical facts like Henry V's marriage to Catherine of Valois (Depp), daughter of France's King Charles VI, as part of a peaceful resolution between the two countries. Adapting the stage play for the Hollywood screen, Michôd and Edgerton also leaned into the Bard's fictional characters, like Henry V's right-hand man Falstaff (played by Edgerton), "a Shakespearian contrivance and a glorious one," Michôd told *EW*. "From the outset, we knew we would be taking some basic scaffolding from Shakespeare, drawing a lot on real history, and then going hog wild with the imagination and engaging in our own grotesque piece of historical revisionism as Shakespeare did." Still, out of respect for the source material, Timothée read Shakespeare's *Henriad* "to be close to them," he told *Screen Rant*. "I wanted to have a strong understanding of the architecture of those plays."

READY FOR WAR: Timothée's most demanding role to date, *The King* required the young actor to train both his mind and his body. Ahead of traveling to England and Hungary for the three-month shoot, he physically bulked up and worked with a dialect coach to learn how to speak like a British monarch during the Middle Ages. But perhaps the greatest challenge was getting into the mindset of one like Henry V, an unconventional ruler at war with his own demons. "I tried to wrap my head around that," Timothée explained to *Vanity Fair*. "As an actor, there's the game of physicality and dialogue and understanding the scope of the story or the tone. But then there's also trying to find that internal life and knowing that it wouldn't be the same as what it would've been today or even fifty years ago."

HAIR APPARENT: *The King* had everyone buzzing, between its epic battle scenes and innovative cinematography—but mostly Timothée's bowl cut. How did the fifteenth-century character end up with a 1990s trend? Turns out, there is only one portrait in existence of Henry V, and that's how the young king's hair is styled. But also, for Michôd, who had "fallen in love" with Timothée's performance in *Call Me by Your Name*, "it felt incredibly important that he undergo[es] a transformation; that the character transform[s] both internally and externally," the director-screenwriter told *Entertainment Weekly*. "I really loved the idea of taking some kind of facsimile of that character from *Call Me by Your Name* and plunking him in the Middle Ages, but then suddenly this monumental burden is placed upon his shoulders and the transformation begins. It felt important to me that the transformation be visible and stark."

BATTLE CRY: An unforgettable scene in *The King* is when Henry must rally his soldiers, who are outnumbered by the French, to victory in the Battle of Agincourt. Walking among men he knows will soon be met with death, the young king implores them to give it their all, culminating with a passionate cry to "Make it impenetrable! Make it yours! Make it England!" Timothée delivered the intense speech at least a dozen times for the cameras, screaming to amplify his voice to the hundreds of extras. "You know, what liberated me as opposed to having the Mel Gibson *Braveheart* impression lingering over the whole shoot, was the idea that Hal . . . isn't so sure of what he's saying himself. There's an insecurity to it," Timothée explained to *Screen Rant*. "So as an actor, especially being from New York and being American, you get to be on that field living out, or playing out, the Battle of Agincourt as Henry V. That was a real gift."

TIMELESS SOUND: One of the many reasons Timothée wanted to work on *The King* was its composer, Nicholas Britell. The three-time Academy Award nominee, best known for *Moonlight*, *The Big Short*, and HBO's *Succession*, "makes the most extraordinary music in movies today," praised Timothée in a discussion with the Academy. Britell truly pushed the envelope for *The King*, eschewing the expected medieval sounds by jumping ahead a thousand years to the twenty-fifth century—and then looking back at the early 1400s "like they were this foreign planet," he explained in the same Q&A session.

    The King is not meant to feel like a period piece, therefore Britell sought to compose a timeless score. He created "strange sounds" by bending metal and playing bass clarinets out of range, which he then ran

through a filter and combined with a traditional string section and boys' choir. The experiment worked so well, Britell admitted, "I'm actually not sure how to pin down the exact harmonic language I was using."

KING OF KINGS: Brad Pitt's Plan B Entertainment produced *The King*, as well as *Beautiful Boy*, and was "super supportive" of both projects. The Academy Award–winning actor visited the set of the 2018 drama and even made an appearance at the Netflix Presents: *The King* event in Hollywood, where he posed for photos with Timothée and the rest of the cast. The A-list association was not lost on the young actor. "I guess I get to say 'Brad Pitt produced both of these,' but that's a really weird thing to say out loud," he joked during an Academy Conversations panel for *The King*.

LITTLE WOMEN
MODERN TAKE ON A TIMELESS CLASSIC
RELEASE DATE: DECEMBER 25, 2019

In nineteenth-century Massachusetts, the March sisters and their dear friend Laurie (Timothée) navigate love and life in a patriarchal society.

DIRECTOR: Greta Gerwig

CAST: Saoirse Ronan, Emma Watson, Florence Pugh, Eliza Scanlen, Laura Dern, Meryl Streep, Chris Cooper

GENRE: Period drama

RATED: PG

BOX OFFICE: $218 million

AWARDS: Academy Awards: Best Picture (nomination)

NEW & IMPROVED: Since 1912, Louisa May Alcott's book has been adapted more than twenty times for the stage, screen, and television. Gerwig's contemporized version focuses the timeline on the beloved March sisters—Meg (Watson), Jo (Ronan), Beth (Scanlen), and Amy (Pugh)—during adulthood, with dialogues inspired by Alcott's follow-up novels in the *Little Women* series. The way they speak is also uncharacteristic for a period piece:

with fast-paced delivery of dialogue meant "to come out of their mouths like they just thought of it, like a heart on your sleeve feeling," Gerwig told GBH. "I didn't want to feel like the lines were embroidered on pillows."

LITTLE MAN: The March sisters are especially close to Theodore "Laurie" Laurence, the complex young man who lives next door with his wealthy grandfather, Mr. Laurence (Cooper). The idealistic dandy would rather travel the world than go into the family business, which makes him "less manly" in the eyes of nineteenth-century aristocracy—yet adored by the little women, particularly tomboy Jo and artist Amy. Laurie's emasculation, Timothée explained to GBH, is not "an absence of the characteristics of the day, but more [of] what he's *not* doing. The tropes and stereotypes about gender or this place in life are not there. Whether because he's young, or doesn't have a lot of social contact, or because he's lucky enough to meet these beautiful (on the inside) women at a young age."

BROTHERLY LOVE: In the classic tale, Laurie is torn between two March sisters: his longtime crush Jo, who rejects his marriage proposal, and the younger Amy, who ultimately accepts. "Laurie and Jo are like two sides of the same coin," Timothée said in an on-set interview, explaining their complicated relationship. "I think they complete each other in a way, certainly in their youth." But as adults, feelings changed. A pivotal scene in *Little Women* is when Jo emphatically tells Laurie, "It would be a disaster if we married," as he begs her to reconsider. Timothée translated what she meant, telling *Harper's Bazaar*, "It's true, people that are socially compatible . . . in their youth, that does not mean that it's meant to be for life." Later in the film, Laurie tells Jo, "You were right" about their incompatibility and reveals he married her sister Amy. Jo's reaction "is my favorite scene of Saoirse's in the movie," said Timothée, "when she collects herself in the doorway before she speaks to [Amy]. I think that's her best."

ART IMITATES LIFE: After working with Timothée in 2017's *Lady Bird*, Gerwig asked him, "Hey, want to do another movie?" The answer was "yes"; however, the young actor had never read *Little Women*, despite it being one of the most popular pieces of American literature. He picked it up immediately to learn more about the March sisters and, of course, Laurie—but Timothée was closer to his character than he thought. "I feel like Laurie's you," Gerwig told him during a joint interview with Rotten Tomatoes. Describing the nineteenth-century character as the "OG ally" for women, "Laurie's a new vision of masculinity . . . and I feel like Timothée as an emerging young person is also doing that."

CHARACTER DEVELOPMENT: Before Timothée, among the notable actors who portrayed Laurie were Peter Lawford, opposite Elizabeth Taylor in 1949, and Christian Bale in the 1994 classic starring Winona Ryder, Kirsten Dunst, Claire Danes, and Susan Sarandon. Twenty-five years later, Gerwig fleshed out the character by revealing more of his personality—and individual impact on each of the four little women. "She gave him real agency, real grounded-ness, vulnerability," Timothée told *Entertainment Tonight*.

TIMELESS TRENDS: In keeping with the renewed spirit of Gerwig's *Little Women*, costume designer Jacqueline Durran put a twentieth-century spin on Civil War–era fashion. For Laurie specifically, she took inspiration from "modern references," like 1960s Bob Dylan—coincidentally who Timothée went on to portray five years later in *A Complete Unknown*—and Teddy Boys, a mid-century British rock-and-roll subculture whose clothing mimicked turn-of-the-century Victorian dandies and the subsequent Edwardian period. Going back even further in time, there are also fashionable nods to 1880s Paris, where Laurie reunites with Amy early in the film.

The character's wardrobe of button-down shirts and vests was tailored for Chalamaniacs, Durran revealed to *Vulture*. "I was looking for a style of suit that would be accessible to a young audience in terms of what they wanted to look at Timothée wearing. I tried to find a way into a look that wasn't alienating." He also lent his own fashion flair to Laurie. "When we were fitting for them, I'd tell him, 'Look at these things, this is what you got, how would you wear it?' That's how we went on and got the flavor of Timothée into the style of the clothes. It was how he chose to style the items. He has a way of wearing things. He's a very iconic kind of boy. He's one of the most stylish people I've ever met."

TAKE TWO: *Little Women* reunited Timothée with Gerwig and Ronan, his *Lady Bird* director and costar, respectively, and he was just as excited to collaborate with the creative duo again. "Saoirse's one of my favorite people I've ever worked with, and I feel like I'm often learning from her," Timothée said in a promotional on-set interview. "Her energies, her talent as an actress, the way she accesses her talent is so palpable." As for Gerwig, "She's an extraordinary human" outside of Hollywood, he gushed to *Extra*. And now that she's crossed over from acting "to tell the stories she wants" as a writer and director, "I want to be a part of that." And she'll gladly take him. "He's one of my favorites," Gerwig confessed to *Extra*. "I can't wait to see what he's gonna make—and I can't wait to try to get him to make more of mine."

DUNE

A LEADING MAN TO SAVE CINEMA
RELEASE DATE: OCTOBER 22, 2021

The sci-fi saga follows Paul Atreides (Timothée) as his noble family battles for control of Arrakis, a desert planet that is the sole source of melange, the most valuable commodity in the universe.

DIRECTOR: Denis Villeneuve

CAST: Zendaya, Rebecca Ferguson, Oscar Isaac, Josh Brolin, Stellan Skarsgård, Javier Bardem

GENRE: Science fiction

RATED: PG-13

BOX OFFICE: $407.6 million

AWARDS: MTV Movie & TV Awards: Best Performance in a Movie (nomination); People's Choice Awards: The Drama Movie Star of 2021 (nomination)

DESTINY'S CHILD: As the son of Duke Leto Atreides (Isaac), Paul reluctantly inherits his family's destiny when the tyrannical House Harkonnen conspires to take control of Arrakis—and his father is killed in the ensuing chaos. It's an overwhelming responsibility for the young character, and one that Timothée could relate to as he took on the largest scale production of his career. "To get to have a big role in [this movie], you're pinching yourself and the imposter syndrome you feel, that's what Paul would be feeling," he revealed to *Variety*. Compounding his anxiety was working with Villeneuve, the acclaimed director of *Sicario*, *Arrival*, and *Blade Runner 2049*, whose experience as a filmmaker Timothée likened to "a carnival that's already in motion. So, it's more your responsibility to just not mess up the turning of the wheel."

Villeneuve, a longtime fan of the *Dune* book series, never once doubted entrusting his passion project to Timothée. But there was one scene—when Paul must pass a deadly Gom Jabbar test of his humanity—that truly convinced the director. "To go through that process of having Timothée diving into that zone of pain and starting to transform himself in front of the camera, it was so impressive for me, and I knew . . . I was like, 'Whoa, we've got a movie.'"

VISION OF LOVE: Throughout *Dune*, Paul is haunted by visions of the future, and in them he sees a mysterious woman with piercing blue eyes: Chani, a warrior who lives on Arrakis, played by Zendaya. Much to the dismay of fans, Zendaya only has seven minutes of screen time—but Timothée assured everyone Chani would have a much greater role in the potential sequel, as their romance is a pivotal piece of Paul's destiny. "They have a lot to do together, let's put it like that," he hinted to *Deadline*.

HOT AS HELL: Filmed in the Middle East, *Dune*'s desert scenes did not need any Hollywood magic—it was brutally hot on the set as temperatures soared into the triple digits. In the book series, the characters wear "stillsuits" intended to cool down the body, but the film's costumes actually had the opposite effect for the actors. "In real life, they make you extra hot," Timothée revealed on *Good Morning America*. "And if you have to go to the bathroom, you kind of have a crisis of conscious . . . you've got to plan your potty breaks."

PARTY LIKE IT'S 10,191: Despite the heaviness of the film, Timothée and the cast of *Dune* kept the mood light on set when they could. Dance parties were a regular occurrence, usually in Zendaya's dressing room, with the lead actor moonlighting as the deejay—and he had a very specific theme for his playlist: a night out in 2008. "Anyone who knows this man knows he travels with sound," Zendaya dished on Timothée to *Good Morning America*. "There's always some kind of music emanating from his pocket or a small speaker that he carries with him. He definitely started with the tunes, I hosted in my dressing room, and then we had a few people attending our little party, one of them being Javier Bardem." The Academy Award–winning actor, who plays Stilgar, leader of the Fremens, "was grooving," Zendaya added on *The Late Show*. "He had the moves."

(NOT) MADE FOR TV: While many big-budget action flicks come to life in postproduction, *Dune* eschewed special effects for practical sets, filmed entirely on location in Jordan and Abu Dhabi. To truly enjoy the spectacle, Timothée and Villeneuve emphatically recommended seeing *Dune* on the big screen. So when the director learned his sci-fi epic's theatrical release would be simultaneously streamed on Max, he was understandably heated.

In an op-ed published by *Variety*, Villeneuve blasted Warner Bros. for the decision—which he found out through the media, not from the studio. "There is absolutely no love for cinema, nor for the audience here. It is all about the survival of a telecom mammoth, one that is currently bearing an astronomical debt of more than $150 billion," he wrote. "Streaming can produce great content, but not movies of *Dune*'s scope and scale. Warner Bros.' decision means *Dune* won't have the chance to perform financially in order to be viable and piracy will ultimately triumph. Warner Bros. might just have killed the *Dune* franchise." Fortunately, scores of moviegoers took Timothée's advice and headed to the theater: *Dune* grossed $407.6 million and ultimately got the green light for a sequel.

FORTNITE X DUNE: Timothée's worlds collided when Paul Atreides was dropped into the popular video game *Fortnite* in 2021. The actor and passionate gamer got his first look at the digitized *Dune* character in an interview with influencer Nate Hill. "Wow, this is one of the trippiest things I've ever seen in my life . . . This is super badass!" He got to play *Fortnite x Dune* for the first time at the London premiere and was just as blown away by the collaboration. "I feel like I'm in the *Twilight Zone*," he joked, "signing all these pictures and now playing *Fortnite*."

TOP HONORS: Although Timothée didn't receive any awards for his portrayal of Paul, *Dune* got the recognition it deserved, winning eighty-nine of its two hundred-plus nominations. At the 2022 Academy Awards, the film took home six Oscars including Best Cinematography, Best Visual Effects, and Best Original Score for Hans Zimmer—who also nabbed a Golden Globe as well as a Grammy nomination.

EMPIRE STATE OF MIND

A fourth-generation native New Yorker, Timmy grew up a quintessential big-city kid—and quickly. By the age of ten, he was riding the subway alone, albeit occasionally "while getting yelled at by naked, crazy people," he reminisced to *Verge*. The Chalamet family home was a two-bedroom apartment on the thirty-third floor of Manhattan Plaza, a federally subsidized housing complex for performing artists, most famously Alicia Keys, James Earl Jones, Larry David, and now, Timothée Chalamet. "It felt like we were literally floating in the sky," he told *ShortList* in 2018 of the artists' colony that has its own supermarket, bank, playground, and swimming pool. Music and singing filled the hallways until 10 p.m. every day during designated rehearsal hours, when Timmy would head to his grandmother's apartment five floors below to practice piano. "My parents had this board we kept under the living room couch that they'd take out when I wanted to tap dance," his sister, Pauline, also an actress, told the *Sydney Morning Herald*. "There was a period of my life where I resented my parents for living in this building full of kooky people . . . Now I'm like, it's not really embarrassing, it was pretty cool."

BONES AND ALL
BLOODY GOOD ROLE TO SINK HIS TEETH INTO
RELEASE DATE: NOVEMBER 23, 2022

Maren (Taylor Russell) and Lee (Timothée), two young people afflicted with cannibalism, bond over their burden on a cross-country road trip.

DIRECTOR: Luca Guadagnino

CAST: Taylor Russell, Michael Shuhlbarg, André Holland, Chloe Sevigny, Mark Rylance

GENRE: Romantic horror

RATED: R

BOX OFFICE: $15.2 million

AWARDS: Venice Film Festival: Golden Lion (nomination), Silver Lion for Best Director; Independent Spirit Awards: Best Feature (nomination)

GUT INSTINCT: When Guadagnino first read the script for *Bones and All*, based on the 2015 novel by Camille DeAngelis, he knew immediately that he wanted Timothée—whom he directed in *Call Me by Your Name*—to play Lee. But would Timothée want to play a cannibal? "We met, and as always it was so profoundly inspiring to talk to him because he's so clever and has such a specific point of view on things," Guadagnino recalled to *Deadline*. "He said to me, 'I'd like to talk to you and [screenwriter David Kajganich] to see where this character should go,' and so a conversation started. That conversation made the character more mature and made the movie more mature in turn." Timothée had a clear vision for Lee, who was "a blast of joy" in the original script. He felt the character—who does not appear in the film until the thirty-three-minute mark—should be more subdued, fragile, and less certain of his hunger for human flesh.

LOVE BITES: *Bones and All* follows two cannibals on a murderous road trip to feed their cravings—but Timothée and Guadagnino insist it's much more a love story than a horror flick. "It's part of our way of expressing our deep passion for something," the director told *Deadline*. "'I love you to death. I will eat you because I love you so much.'" Timothée put it a bit more poetically. He explained to *Indulge* magazine that he felt "their eating condition" was a metaphor for either childhood trauma (Maren had been abandoned by her mother as an infant) or addiction, "or just carrying something you can't quite make sense of, or something you carry shame with."

Timothée, also a producer of the film, developed the script with Guadagnino and his team during the peak of COVID-19 in the fall of 2020, which influenced a recurring theme of isolation. "His biggest vulnerability, like a lot of people's vulnerabilities when they spend so much time alone, is true love, real love," Timothée told *Indulge*. "So, when he finds that with Maren, it's his greatest strength in many ways, it's the opening of the colors of the universe he has never got to experience, but it's also . . . the hardest thing for him to go through because those moments when you're able to fall for someone else, is when you look more closely in the mirror. And what he sees is terrifying."

SWEET TOOTH: As an actor, Timothée has had to do a lot of interesting things on camera—but eating the flesh of another human being is in a disturbing class all its own. Luckily, it was much sweeter than it looked: the body parts he and Russell feasted on during the film's gory scenes was a concoction of maraschino cherries, dark chocolate, and Fruit Roll-Ups.

SEEING RED: Timothée's famous hair underwent its most colorful transformation to portray Lee. Cut into a mullet, his brown locks were dyed red, a symbolic color—but not because it relates to blood; instead, it served as a reflection of the energy of the character: "We were thinking about the color of the period and strong, crazy colors like Cyndi Lauper, the more iconic rock stars," *Bones and All* hair designer Massimo Gattabrusi told *PopSugar*. The two-hour process began with bleaching Timothée's hair but leaving his roots dark "to feel the time pass through the hair." Several shades of red were tested before settling on a "really strong" copper color using semipermanent dye.

Timothée viewed Lee's hair as a storytelling tool; as the vibrancy of the red naturally faded over the course of filming, he and Gattabrusi timed touch-ups so the color was subtly intense in specific scenes. "When I saw the movie, you don't [notice] this change in color, and that's what I wanted," noted Gattabrusi. "It's just something that you feel in the background. You don't see it, but you feel it."

ON THE FRINGE: *Silence of the Lambs* fans might recognize Maren's unique hairstyle. Her micro-bangs were an homage to a minor character in Jonathan Demme's 1991 cult classic: Stacy Hubka, who is interviewed by Clarice (Jodie Foster) about the murder of her friend. Guadagnino knew he wanted his leading lady to wear her hair the same, and Russell allowed Gattabrusi to make the chop right then and there when they first met to discuss Maren's appearance in the film.

GRUESOME TWOSOME: Maren and Lee's true romance inspired the film's composers, Trent Reznor and Atticus Ross, who wrote several songs inspired by the cannibal couple, notably "(You Made It Feel) Like Home" featuring the Nine Inch Nails frontman on vocals. Heard at the end of the film, "I think it's devastating when that song comes in," Ross told *The Wrap*. "I know I can speak for us both when I say we fell in love with those characters and with that particular moment with those particular lyrics, the imagery and the sparseness."

FINANCIAL KILLER: *Bones and All* premiered at the 2022 Venice Film Festival, where it received a ten-minute standing ovation. Critics around the world agreed with Timothée and Guadagnino, praising the film's love story and artful telling through a couple of cannibals. However, when the film was released in theaters, it was a box-office bloodbath: *Bones and All* grossed millions of dollars less than its budget, a disappointment that was attributed to the ongoing pandemic and its impact on the movie-going experience.

WONKA

THE SWEETEST ROLE OF HIS CAREER
RELEASE DATE: DECEMBER 15, 2023

Fifty years after *Willy Wonka & the Chocolate Factory*, its prequel follows the candy man's rise to fame—but first, he must triumph over the villainous Chocolate Cartel.

DIRECTOR: Paul King

CAST: Hugh Grant, Olivia Colman, Calah Lane, Keegan-Michael Key, Patterson Joseph, Matt Lucas, Rowan Atkinson, Sally Hawkins

GENRE: Musical fantasy comedy

RATED: PG

BOX OFFICE: $632.3 million

AWARDS: Nickelodeon Kids Choice Awards: Favorite Movie Actor; Golden Globe Awards: Best Actor (nomination)

PURE IMAGINATION: Timothée is the third actor to portray Willy Wonka, following in the footsteps of Gene Wilder in the 1971 original and Johnny Depp in Tim Burton's 2005 remake. For his version of the iconic candymaker, in his younger years when he's still a bright-eyed optimist,

Timothée was inspired by King's "heartfelt" origins story. "I remember reading the script and immediately understanding that one of the crucial aspects of the character was his undying spirit and ambition," the star told *USA Today*. "It was a total inverse of that Willy Wonka with a demented look in his eye that we all know. How would that character have started to land in a place where he's still childlike but sort of broken?"

King, who previously directed the live-action *Paddington* films, came up with the Wonka origins story and also wrote its screenplay. "I had this idea of a young man trying to be Willy Wonka, but he's not quite there," he told *USA Today*. "His hat's battered, his overcoat's tattered and there's holes in his boots. He's like Charlie Chaplin in that movie *The Immigrant*, in the sense that he's coming to a new world with hopes and dreams." To get into character, King suggested Timothée watch the films of another Old Hollywood legend, Frank Capra, to channel the joyful spirit of Wonka "and what a good soul can do in a corrupt world."

SWEET & SOUR: Twenty-five years before Charlie Bucket, Veruca Salt, Mike Teavee, Violet Beauregarde, and Augustus Gloop, *Wonka*'s origin story does feature a few familiar faces, like his onetime rival, Slugworth (Joseph), and an Oompa Loompa named Lofty (Grant). The rest of the 2023 cast is comprised of brand-new characters: the people who influenced Willy's chocolatier journey. His assistant is an orphan girl named Noodle (Lane), who helps him go up against the powerful Chocolate Cartel, a group of businessmen threatened by Wonka's superior product. To take down the rising candy-maker, the villains bribe chocolate-addicted community leaders such as the chief of police (Key) and the cleric (Atkinson).

MUSIC MAN: *Wonka* is Timothée's first onscreen musical, but the lifelong performer is no stranger to a little song and dance. In high school, he had starring roles in *Sweet Charity* and *Cabaret*, yet "it felt like a muscle I had never fully developed," he admitted to *USA Today*. "I had been around musical theater my whole life, and it's different doing it on film. But there was a learning curve to that, which was very rewarding." To get up to "movie standard" for *Wonka*'s many musical numbers, Timothée went through months of training with Tony Award–winning choreographer Cristopher Gattelli who taught him how to tap dance.

GOLDEN AGE: There are no golden tickets in *Wonka*, but there's plenty of Golden Age. As the film takes place twenty-five years before the 1971 original, we enter the late 1940s, "the golden age of the Hollywood musical," King explained to the British Film Institute. "I love my postwar musicals. It didn't take much to convince me to go and spend some evenings researching those old movies." Fred Astaire, best remembered for his musical comedies with Ginger Rogers, especially influenced "For a Moment," a Wonka-Noodle duet that takes the two dreamers on a sky-high tour of London. "There's an ease to Fred Astaire," King described to *Letterboxd*. "I mean, *Royal Wedding*, where he dances on the roof of the cabin, I love that sense of turning gravity off. There's another sequence . . . he's dancing on the rooftops and bouncing off bits of the building. That was a real reference for our sequence with Willy and Noodle and the balloons."

BLAST FROM THE PAST: There are several nods to the 1971 film in *Wonka*: Hoverchocs candy has the same effect as Fizzy Lifting Drink;

Willy nearly drowns in a vat of chocolate like Augustus; and Lofty borrows Wilder's famous dismissal, "Good day, sir!" Much to Timothée's dismay, there's one homage they couldn't quite get right. In the original, Wonka makes a memorable entrance when his cane gets stuck in a sidewalk and he stumbles, then rolls into a perfect somersault. Fifty years later, the prequel filmmakers struggled to pull off the same stunt. "We tried in the opening chocolate store sequence," Timothée confessed to BBC Radio 1. The roll itself was "nearly impossible to accomplish," but the cane sticking proved more difficult. "We put a magnet on the bottom of the cane and then a magnet on the floor . . . We figured in the original, they must have built a tiny hole in the ground or something."

CANDY IS DANDY: Six years and twelve roles since his debut in *Call Me by Your Name*, Timothée declared *Wonka* his favorite of all his films. "It is the most fun I've had working on anything ever," he gushed on *The Graham Norton Show*. "It is sweet and good and will fill you with joy." His parents wholeheartedly agreed. "This is my mom and dad's favorite project I've ever been in. They're thrilled," Timothée told *USA Today*. "My mom has been encouraging me to do a play for the last ten, twelve years. And my dad, too, he goes, 'Wow. There's a smile on your face, finally.'"

EVERLASTING BLOCKBUSTER: *Wonka* was such a global success, there was immediate talk for a sequel. The prequel's ending certainly left the door open to continue the story: Willy daydreams about his own chocolate factory while singing the 1971 theme song "Pure Imagination." Although *Charlie and the Chocolate Factory* author Roald Dahl didn't write about this particular period of Wonka's life, King revealed there was plenty of material to pull from in Dahl's archives. "I would definitely like to do more. And I'd like to spend more time in this world," the director teased in *Total Film* magazine. "Dahl was definitely interested in taking Willy Wonka on. There's drafts that didn't really go anywhere, and there's a short story. He didn't really write sequels, but this was the one book where he clearly felt there was more in the tank there. There's an awful lot more Wonka story that we have that we would like to tell."

DUNE: PART TWO
TIMOTHÉE'S FIRST OFFICIAL BLOCKBUSTER
RELEASE DATE: MARCH 1, 2024

In the sequel, Paul immerses himself in Fremen culture and falls in love with Chani (Zendaya), only to betray her in his quest for revenge, and ultimately, power.

DIRECTOR: Denis Villeneuve

CAST: Zendaya, Rebecca Ferguson, Josh Brolin, Austin Butler, Florence Pugh, Christopher Walken, Lea Seydoux, Javier Bardem

GENRE: Science fiction

RATED: PG-13

BOX OFFICE: $711.8 million

AWARDS: Critics Choice Awards: Best Picture (nomination); Golden Globes: Best Motion Picture (nomination)

NEW BLOOD: The saga of Paul Atreides continues in the *Dune* sequel, with a few new faces. Butler plays the sadistic Feyd-Rautha, nephew to Baron Harkonnen, who becomes the new ruler of Arrakis—and unleashes his fury on the planet in his hunt for Paul. The House Atreides heir is on a warpath of his own, avenging his father's death by taking the throne from

Emperor Saddam IV (Walken), as well as his daughter Irulan (Pugh). In an uncredited cameo, Anya-Taylor Joy portrays Alia, Paul's unborn sister who appears in his visions.

LEADING MAN: Filmed three years after *Dune*, Timothée returned to the set for the sequel older and wiser, just like his character who was a teenager in the first film. Villeneuve especially noticed the actor was more trained for fight sequences and disciplined in general. "You know, when you are the lead on a movie, there's a presence, the way you approach your work and your discipline will necessarily have a ripple effect on the rest of the crew," the director told *GQ*. "He was the first one on set, always ready. And I was super pleased and impressed with how Timothée really embraced that discipline and became, for me, a real leading actor on this film."

A CAUTIONARY TALE: To win over the skeptical people of Arrakis, Paul's mother Jessica (Ferguson) tries to convince the Fremen that her son is the prophet they've long awaited. As the film progresses, Paul—who is now having visions of a holy war fought in his name—seems to believe it too. "This is a warning against religious fanaticism, and worship of leaders or charisma, like we see all too commonly in the world today," Timothée told *SFX* magazine. "Because it's tempting, and it's an easy way out. This is very much a cautionary tale, which isn't obvious because perhaps when you think sci-fi or you think popular story, we think of the obvious figures of hero and villain. You wouldn't necessarily think there's a central figure that's something of a hero, but what's called of him is villainous. I think this movie walks that line very, very carefully and closely."

SURF & TURF: Arrakis is inhabited by sandworms, massive 1,300-foot-long (396 m) creatures with razor-sharp teeth that can burrow into the desert sand. In his assimilation into the Fremen culture, Paul becomes a sandrider, using a maker hook to snag a worm and travel across the desert. The two-minute sequence took the Worm Unit of special-effects artists four months to create. So how did they do it? "Obviously the worm wasn't there on the day, so there's a certain process of visualization," Timothée joked on Fandango's *Big Ticket Interview*. In its place, the team built a life-size portion of the sandworm where he could act out hooking it.

As for the ride, that proved trickier. "There's a technique to it. I remember going to Z and, you know, wishing that my arm technique was different," he said with a laugh. As Zendaya explained, they had no frame of reference on how to properly sand-ride, "so you're trying to do it cool and make it look strong. 'Do I hold like this? Do I stand like this? Do I have my leg here?' You're trying to have the strongest worm-riding pose."

SECRET LANGUAGE: On the set, Timothée got to practice his French with Villeneuve, a native of Quebec, the French-speaking province of Canada. "It was the way that we were able to find intimacy in the chaos," the director told the *Los Angeles Times*. "It was our protected landscape. A second secret language."

CRUISE CONTROL: During the making of *Part Two*, a different kind of sequel arrived in theaters: *Top Gun: Maverick*. While in Budapest for principal photography, Timothée went to see Tom Cruise's aviation blockbuster—and became so obsessed, he returned to the theater seven more times. Once, he rented out the entire ninety-seat cinema (for two dollars a pop) and brought along the *Dune* cast and crew. "*Top Gun* was just hugely inspiring to me last summer when we were making *Dune*," Timothée told *GQ* in 2023. "Some of the crew were kind of scoffing at going, but I just thought it was one of the greatest films I've ever seen." By February 2024, he admitted to *ExtraTV* that he had seen *Top Gun: Maverick* "twelve or thirteen times."

PART THREE: At the end of *Part Two*, Paul's story was just beginning. *Dune* author Frank Hebert wrote a second novel, *Dune Messiah*—and Villeneuve is developing an adaptation of that as well. "*Dune Messiah* was written in reaction to the fact that people perceived Paul Atreides as a hero, which is not what he wanted to do," the director explained to *Empire* magazine. "My adaptation is closer to his idea that it's actually a warning." Hans Zimmer, who composed the scores of *Part One* and *Part Two*, also confirmed in 2024 that he is writing music for *Part Three*.

Timothée certainly seems eager to reprise his role. During the promotion of *Part Two*, he talked about the sequel's depiction of Paul's villainous heroism. "If we're lucky to do *Messiah*, a third one, I think we'll explore it even more successfully," he told the *Los Angeles Times*. "I think this movie would have to have a certain amount of success for that to happen. But we'd be very motivated to do one, to do *Messiah*." The rest of the cast is on board for a third installment as well. "Any time Denis calls, it's a 'yes' from me," Zendaya said on *The Big Ticket*. "I'm excited to see what happens."

WHEN TIMMY MET MARTY

In 2024, Timothée starred in an ad campaign for the Bleu de Chanel fragrance directed by the one and only Martin Scorsese. The black-and-white clip illustrates "an actor's conflict between celebrity and staying true to himself." From the moment Timothée wakes up in New York City, it's a nonstop grind of paparazzi, interviews, and overzealous fans. Hinting at the perfume's name, he's distracted by the color blue—and ultimately, a mystery woman on a subway platform. "It should've occurred to me sooner that I try to find something to work on with him," Timothée said of Scorsese, who's been nominated for sixteen Academy Awards for films including *Raging Bull*, *Goodfellas*, and *The Wolf of Wall Street*. "Yes, it's a perfume ad, but for me it was an opportunity for an enormous education." Scorsese learned a lot, too. "The thing about sixty seconds is it's harder [than a feature film]," he told Timothée in a conversation for *GQ*. "Every frame counts . . . I find these much more intense, they're real workouts."

A COMPLETE UNKNOWN
MAKE-OR-BREAK DEFINING MOMENT
RELEASE DATE: DECEMBER 25, 2024

Singer-songwriter Bob Dylan changed music history in 1965 when he put down his acoustic guitar to go "electric" at the Newport Folk Festival.

DIRECTOR: James Mangold

CAST: Elle Fanning, Edward Norton, Monica Barbaro

GENRE: Biographical drama

RATED: R

BOX OFFICE: $46.33 million

AWARDS: Golden Globes: Best Motion Picture (nomination); SAG Awards: Outstanding Performance by a Male Actor in a Leading Role (nomination)

METHOD MAN: Timothée always throws himself into a role, but to portray iconic singer-songwriter Bob Dylan, he had to fully immerse himself in "Bob World": he listened to his music, read his memoir, met with experts on the 1960s folk scene, spent time at his old haunts in Manhattan's Greenwich Village, and even rented a home in Woodstock, New York, decked out in Dylan memorabilia. And the actor didn't let up when *A Complete Unknown*—originally titled *Going Electric*—was shelved for three years due to the COVID-19 pandemic and 2023 Hollywood labor strikes, and nearly canceled altogether. "I haven't stopped preparing, which has been one of the greatest gifts for me," Timothée revealed to *Variety* in 2022. "It's been a wonderful experience getting to dive into that world, whether we get to make [the film] or not."

BECOMING BOB: Timothée was so impressed with how his *Dune: Part Two* costar Austin Butler embodied Elvis in his 2022 biopic (which earned the actor an Academy Award nomination), he hired the same team to transform him into Bob Dylan, training daily with vocal coach Eric Vetro and movement coach Polly Bennett. "He does everything with such a playful air," Vetro told *GQ* about Timothée, "but there's always that core of real seriousness where he is gonna nail it. It's taking on all the characteristics of Dylan's voice and his mannerisms and his speech patterns, and bringing that into the music—so that when you hear Timothée do the music, what you're really getting is the *essence* of Bob Dylan. You're not getting an impersonation of him. It's breathing new life into that voice that we know so well."

DYLAN & FRIENDS: Although the film was originally promoted as "a Bob Dylan biopic," *A Complete Unknown* focuses on a specific period in the folk singer-songwriter's life in the early 1960s as he was coming up in the Greenwich Village music scene, until he made the controversial switch to electrically amplified instrumentation in 1965 at the Newport Folk Festival. Based on the 2015 book, *Dylan Goes Electric* by Elijah Wald, the adaptation features many of his famous friends during the era, including Johnny Cash (Boyd Holbrook), Bob Seeger (Norton), and Joan Baez (Barbaro).

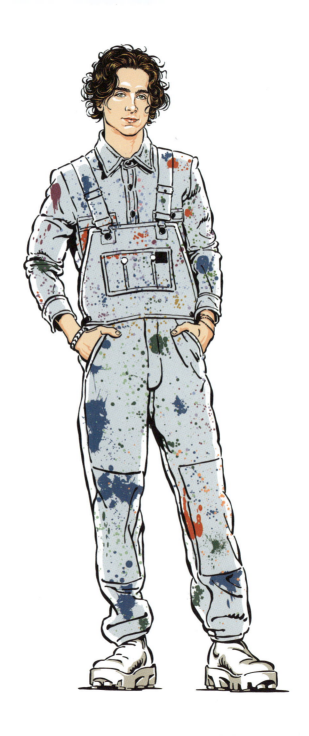

A Complete Unknown traces back to when seventeen-year-old Dylan hitchhiked from Minnesota to New York with only sixteen dollars in his pocket. He wanted to meet folk icon Woody Guthrie (Scoot McNairy), who was in the hospital battling the neurodegenerative Huntington's disease. Dylan found him—and the rest is history. "He sings Woody a song that he wrote for him and befriends Pete Seeger, who is like a son to Woody," Mangold recounted on the *Happy, Sad, Confused* podcast, "and Pete sets him up with gigs at local clubs and there you meet Joan Baez and all these other people who are part of this world, and this wanderer who comes in from Minnesota with a fresh name and a fresh outlook on life, becomes a star, signs to the biggest record company in the world within a year, and three years later, has record sales rivaling The Beatles."

MUSICAL MUSE: Fanning plays Sylvie Russo, a fictional character based on Dylan's real-life girlfriend at the time, Suze Rotolo, who inspired several songs on his seminal 1963 album, *The Freewheelin' Bob Dylan*. The university student and artist is immortalized on the cover, an iconic image of the couple arm in arm as they walk down snow-covered Jones Street in Greenwich Village—a scene that is recreated in *A Complete Unknown*. Rotolo and her left-wing family had a major influence on Dylan politically. It wasn't until the couple met in 1961 that his songs evolved into social commentary on issues like the civil rights movement.

A feminist who resented being known as the famous singer's "chick," Rotolo ended the relationship in 1964, after Dylan had an affair with Baez. His bitterness inspired the song "Ballad in Plain D," which lyrically eviscerated Rotolo's "parasite" sister whom he blamed for the breakup.

Four decades later, Rotolo broke her silence on Dylan in her memoir, which Fanning read to prepare for her role.

BOB'S BLESSING: Timothée didn't get to meet Dylan, but he did get his blessing. Mangold spent "several, wonderfully charming days in his company, just one-on-one, talking to him," the director revealed on the *Happy, Sad, Confused* podcast in 2023. The "supportive" singer, who's also a bit of a movie buff, went over the script and annotated his feedback on the pages—which Mangold is keeping as a treasured relic.

OPINIONS THEY ARE A-CHANGIN': *A Complete Unknown* was shot on location in New Jersey—and the paparazzi were right there to document it all. Social media's reaction to seeing Timothée in character was mixed, but opinions changed after fans got their first official look—and listen—at the actor as Bob Dylan in the trailer for *A Complete Unknown* in July 2024. "The Dylan community was pretty skeptical," Craig Danuloff, host of the *Dylan.FM* podcast, told *Variety*. "Now I'd say about ninety percent of the fans on X—and they'll complain about anything—are very positive about the trailer." Anne Margaret Daniel, a professor teaching a class on Dylan at The New School, applauded Timothée's indisputable dedication to the role. "The way he strums, the way his right hand is moving on the strings, is perfect. He's obviously watched a lot of footage of Bob performing."

EASTER EGG: Timothée spent so long in "Bob World," that the singer-songwriter influenced another iconic character he portrayed on the big screen: Willy Wonka. While recording a song for the 2023 musical, he momentarily slipped into Dylan's voice to give a nod to his 1963 song

"A Hard Rain's A-Gonna Fall." "'There's a lyric in 'A World of Your Own,' where Willy goes, 'There's a hard rain that's gonna fall.' And I really couldn't resist doing it [as Dylan]," Timothée revealed to *USA Today*. "It was totally improper, but I was dying for it to be stuck in there. It's one of the lines that we had to rerecord."

PART THREE

Chalamania

TIMOTHÉE
A TO Z

Timothée is as complex as the characters he brings to life on the big screen—but he also enjoys the simple things in life. A native New Yorker, he survives on bagels, had his first kiss in Times Square, and is a diehard fan of the New York Knicks basketball team. The Oscar-nominated actor also has a little-known past as a high school rapper named Lil Timmy Tim and an Xbox 360 influencer on YouTube. These are the fun facts every certified Chalamaniac should know.

ASTROLOGICAL SIGN

Born on December 27, 1995, Timmy is a Capricorn: ambitious, hardworking, determined, and sensitive—all the characteristics that make him one of Hollywood's most respected (and award-winning) young actors. According to his birth chart, which is based on the precise moment he entered the world at 9:16 p.m., four of his ruling planets (Mars, Mercury, Neptune, and Uranus) also fall under Capricorn and are concentrated in his fifth house, most often linked to creativity and self-expression.

In astrology, one's rising sign relates to the "first impression" they make on others. Timmy's is Virgo, an ever-improving perfectionist who often seeks out mentorship—which he's done with several veteran actors, including the star of the film that first inspired him: Christian Bale. On the set of the 2017 Western drama *Hostiles*, "I picked his brain quite a bit about *The Dark Knight*," Timmy told *Time Out*, "but even more so about *American Psycho*, because I'm crazy about that performance." The inner Timmy is guided by his moon sign, Pisces, a dreamer who can turn fantasy into reality.

In love, he's a thoughtful dater. With his Mars in Capricorn, he craves tradition yet is perfectly fine with being single until he finds the one. Is it any coincidence that Kylie Jenner, a passionate Leo, is a Capricorn rising?

BAGELS

You can take the boy out of New York, but you can't take New York out of the boy—Timothée loves the quintessential Big Apple breakfast: a bagel. His go-to order is an everything bagel with bacon, egg, and cheese from Tompkins Square Bagels in the East Village. The actor's obsession is so well-known, there are countless TikToks devoted to Tompkins Square Bagels (or TSB) pilgrimages just to taste-test his favorite bagel. Timothée's

Dune: Part Two costars weren't aware, however. During a Q&A with *Vanity Fair* in 2024, Zendaya, Florence Pugh, Austin Butler, and Josh Brolin all failed to guess his order correctly. "Man, no New Yorkers on this cast," sighed Timothée. "Sorry to everyone on the East Coast."

He showed some hometown hospitality at *The King* premiere, when the film's star arrived on the red carpet with the hottest accessory, a white bag . . . filled with bagels. When Timothée learned fans had been waiting for hours outside the SVA Theater just to catch a glimpse of him, he made a pit stop at Tompkins Square Bagels to bring them sustenance. In the essence of time, the bagels were without his go-to bacon, egg, and cheese, but everyone was satisfied nonetheless.

How much does Timothée love bagels? Despite his French heritage, he prefers the ring-shaped bread roll over the buttery flaky goodness of a croissant, he admitted to *Vulture*. "Bagels are about ninety-five percent of this diet right here. They keep me alive."

CLUB CHALAMET

Timmy's fans are as passionate as he is talented, but one Chalamaniac in particular has become well-known for going above and beyond with their fervor. Club Chalamet, a superfan account on Instagram and X run by a fifty-something woman named Simone, regularly posts updates on all things Timmy. "I want to help carve out a niche fanbase of mature, well-balanced adults in support of his career," Simone told Refinery29.

But when his romance with Kylie Jenner became public in 2023, @ClubChalamet notoriously had a virtual meltdown, claiming the relationship was fake and had been orchestrated by the reality star's PR-minded mother, Kris Jenner. After the couple was seen kissing at a

Beyoncé concert in Los Angeles, @ClubChalamet hosted an emergency X Spaces gathering to discuss the situation that had left fans "absolutely devastated and disappointed." Of all the things @ClubChalmet had said about Timmy and Kylie, one comment made the superfan go super viral: "We've never even seen them go to Olive Garden," said Simone. "He loves Italian food. I mean, why not just go to Olive Garden?"

Chalamaniacs and social media users alike teased @ClubChalamet relentlessly for the Olive Garden reference, as well as her overzealous "stan" behavior. But arguably, she got the last laugh: three months later at the *Wonka* premiere in Los Angeles, Timothée made a beeline for Simone in a group of fans and posed for a selfie with his most famous fan—which of course she posted on @ClubChalamet. "I was very lucky," she wrote on Instagram, "and I think after the events of recent months, it was a nice karmic scenario for both me and Timothée."

DUAL CITIZENSHIP

Thanks to his American mother and French father, Timothée is legally a citizen of both countries! Born in the US, he spent each summer with his paternal grandparents in Le Chambon-sur-Lignon, a tiny village in France, where he coached youth soccer (ages six to ten) at a camp as a teen. "That time spent there was very formative, even if it also gave rise to a slightly strange phenomenon," he told *La Press* in 2017. "Once I was there, I became the French version of myself. I was completely immersed in the culture and I even dreamed in French. Then I would go back home to New York, and it was as if I was then seized by a kind of identity ambiguity. That said, it gave me a tremendous creative freedom, in that being familiar with another culture gives me additional tools to practice my profession."

Timothée is fluent in French and spoke it at home with his father, Marc Chalamet, growing up, "but it's not a language I have as much command over," he admitted to *VMan* magazine. His sister, Pauline, who also holds dual citizenship, is so comfortable speaking French that she's been living in Paris since 2014.

EDGAR SCISSORHANDS

Super Bowl commercials are arguably more entertaining than the football game, and in 2021 one of the most buzzed-about spots advertised the forthcoming electric crossover, Cadillac Lyriq—starring Timothée as Edward Scissorhands' son, Edgar. Johnny Depp, who portrayed Edward in Tim Burton's 1991 gothic classic, doesn't make an appearance in the commercial, but Winona Ryder did reprise her role as Kim, now the mother of a child with the same affliction as his father of scissor blades for hands. And just like Edward, Edgar struggles in the real world: he can't catch a football without puncturing it—nor can he drive. But luckily, the Cadillac Lyriq is equipped with GM's Super Cruise function, advertised as the first true hands-free driving-assistance technology. The commercial ends with Kim surprising Edgar with a brand-new Lyriq, which he drives off into the sunset in true cinematic fashion.

Timothée was thrilled to honor a film he adored growing up, while also promoting a car that places emphasis on environmental sustainability. Cadillac was electrified by the collaboration, too: the sixty-second Super Bowl ad cost $11 million, and it turned out to be worth every penny. "Timothée has the grace of a silent movie comedian," director David Shane told *AdAge*, "and I thought it was dope that we could help him show off that side."

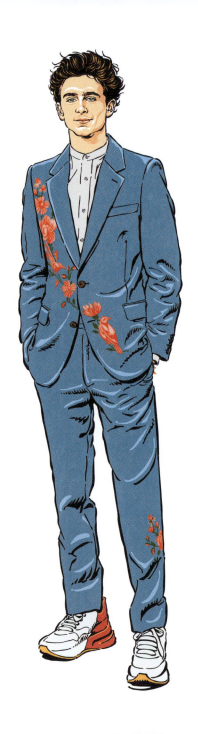

FIRST KISS

Timothée's first kiss sounds like a scene straight out of a rom-com, however, more comedic than romantic. When he was a freshman in high school, the New Yorker was riding in one of the famous glass elevators at the Marriott Marquis in Times Square with a girl he liked. As they ascended the fifty stories, he noticed she was applying Burt's Bees chapstick, so he took it as a hint to do the same. When they reached the top, overlooking the atrium lobby, he went in for a kiss. "I remember I told her that it wasn't my first time. I was just so nervous that she wouldn't be able to tell it wasn't my first time," Timothée recalled to *W Magazine* in 2017. "It was a total shit show. She was my girlfriend for about a month, as these things go in high school. And I think she got sick of me and we didn't talk for four years, just steadfastly avoided each other in the hallways."

GUILTY PLEASURES

Timothée has no shame about the things he loves—*The Office*, Kid Cudi (real name: Scott Mescudi), bacon and eggs on a bagel—still there are a few things he keeps somewhat on the down-low. But all you need to do is ask and he'll gladly spill. During an appearance on the French television show *Quotidien*, the *Beautiful Boy* actor admitted his current guilty-pleasure song was Mariah Carey's "Giving Me Life," a hypnotic jam featuring rapper Slick Rick and English singer-producer Blood Orange. And he proved it by lip-synching the lyrics as the audience clapped along. Timothée can also quote the original *Mean Girls* line for line. His favorite is the weather report from airhead Karen (Amanda Seyfried), who predicts "there's a thirty percent chance it's already raining" while standing outside in a downpour.

Just like millions of others, Timothée can't resist a McDonald's craving. His go-to order is a ten-piece chicken McNuggets with extra-large fries (dipped in barbecue sauce and ketchup), washed down with a fountain drink of Coca-Cola. The native New Yorker is also hooked on West Coast institution In-N-Out Burger, a fast-food chain famous for its "animal-style" burgers and hand-cut fries. In June 2024, Timothée was spotted on a late-night run at an In-N-Out in Sherman Oaks, just a few miles from his Beverly Hills home. When he'd rather stay in and snack, he can look no further than his freezer, which is stocked with Trader Joe's Tarte D'Alsace, a flatbread with crème fraîche, ham, caramelized onions, and Gruyère cheese—how very French of him! For a sweet treat, the *Wonka* star sticks to the basics: Milk Duds, Raisinets, Junior Mints, and Sour Patch Kids (preferably watermelon flavor).

HAIR HYSTERIA

Never has a head of hair had such a grip on pop culture since Jennifer Aniston's "The Rachel" on *Friends*—that is until Timmy. Timothée's effortlessly tousled look has inspired countless YouTube tutorials, evolution photo galleries, film rankings (based on his hair's performance), and journalistic achievements such as a 2021 *New Yorker* article titled "Timothée Chalamet Saves the Universe Because the Future Needs Great Hair." In 2024, NBC's *Today With Hoda & Jenna* devoted an entire segment to "The Timothée." "Are men putting on extensions?" wondered cohost Jenna Bush Hager. "Because you can't just ask for that, you have to grow it."

So what's the secret to Timothée's hair? "There really isn't one," he disappointedly told *Vogue* in 2023. "When I wake up, it's a roll of the dice."

However, in the same interview, the heartthrob admitted that he had a personal "groomer," Jamie Taylor, who was recommended by Channing Tatum, interestingly not someone known for their hair. Taylor has yet to dish on her most famous client, but she has given the world a special gift: a "Timothée C" highlight reel on her Instagram profile loaded with dozens of iconic looks from over the years.

INSTAGRAM

Timothée may be a Gen Z icon, but when it comes to public sharing on social media, he's more of a Baby Boomer. On Instagram, he has nearly 20 million followers to whom he reveals very little. The actor's content is mostly promotion for his films—the first trailer for *A Complete Unknown*, a *Wonka* poster, and behind-the-scenes *Bones and All* photos with costar Taylor Russell. When he does post the occasional selfie, it does numbers: a close-up photo of his eye garnered 4.9 million likes. Scroll far back enough and there are some glimpses of private life: a breakfast of bacon and eggs, celebrating his twenty-second birthday with his grandmother, and his 2014 Instagram debut of a pair of pigeons nuzzling outside his bedroom window juxtaposed with New York City skyscrapers.

Timothée made headlines in 2022 when he slammed social media at a Venice Film Festival press conference for *Bones and All*, which is set in the 1980s and therefore devoid of cell phones and the internet. "It was a relief to play characters who are wrestling with an internal dilemma absent the ability to go on Reddit, X, Instagram, or TikTok and figure out where they fit in," said Timothée. "I think it's hard to be alive now. I think societal collapse is in the air. That's why hopefully this movie will matter."

JOURNALING

For Timothée, it's been a meteoric rise to fame, and since the beginning he's made a concerted effort to document each major milestone along the way. In 2017, as *Call Me by Your Name* and *Lady Bird* positioned him as the next big thing, "Somebody said to me, 'You should keep a journal of this period in your life and really write down this stuff,'" he remarked in an interview with the *Los Angeles Times*. "But that makes me a little uneasy. When I try to appreciate something, it feels like my hands are around the moment, trying to squeeze it." By the following year, however, he had taken the advice and revealed to *i-D* magazine that he was jotting down his self-reflections. "Gratitude and appreciating where you are is very important to me," Timothée explained. "I have about a year and half of work coming up now; I'm doing *Little Women* and *Dune* . . . and I hope I can take time to appreciate it all. What comforts me is that when I wake up, within healthy boundaries, I always have a subtle feeling of gratitude."

Five years later, Timothée revealed he was still on his journaling journey while promoting *Wonka*, his biggest blockbuster to date. During an appearance on *The Drew Barrymore Show*, the star said he wrote "as much as possible" and honored Barrymore's request to write something in her own gratitude journal. He kept it simple—and a true reflection of their conversation, as his curmudgeonly costar Hugh Grant ridiculed the "absurd" idea: "Grateful to be sitting on a couch with Hugh Grant and Drew Barrymore."

KYLIE JENNER

Like his acting roles, Timothée doesn't have a "type" when it comes to the opposite sex. In high school, he dated fellow LaGuardia student Lourdes

Leon, Madonna's daughter, who later revealed that he was her first-ever boyfriend. It would be another five years until the actor was again publicly linked to someone: Lily-Rose Depp, his onscreen love interest in *The King*, whom he dated from September 2018 to April 2020. That summer, he rebounded with *Baby Driver* actress Eiza González.

In April 2023, social media erupted over rumors that Timothée was secretly dating reality star and mother of two, Kylie Jenner. For months, the two dodged paparazzi as they hung out in and around Los Angeles. When they did finally go public that September, it was epic: making out at a Beyoncé concert. After that, the couple popped up hand in hand at the US Open in New York and Paris Fashion Week, and they also celebrated each other's achievements—Timothée beamed with pride as Kylie was honored at the 2023 Innovator Awards, and she attended the LA premiere of *Wonka* (with her mother Kris Jenner as her plus-one). Their PDA peaked at the 2024 Golden Globes, where the Actor in a Musical or Comedy nominee only had eyes for his girlfriend, who reportedly mouthed "I love you" to him during a commercial break. An insider told *People* magazine at the time that Kylie had become "very content, relaxed and focused" since dating Timothée. "Her family loves him."

LIL TIMMY TIM

Timothée is a triple threat: actor, singer . . . rapper? Back in 2013, the LaGuardia High School senior used the right side of his brain for a statistics class project, writing a rap song under the persona "Lil Timmy Tim." But he had quite a big personality, as seen in the student-made accompanying music video: dressed in a gray T-shirt, low-slung jeans, and a backward red baseball cap, Lil Timmy Tim sways from side to side as he

spits lyrics like, "Let's do a problem, let us see / the probability you see me on TV / one-zero-zero-zero trillion percent / I'm a statistical wonder, a statistical gem."

Lil Timmy Tim's math skills may be arguable, but he was correct that he would go on to become a successful actor. However, at the time—four years before *Call Me by Your Name*—he bombed with "Statistics." His teacher, Ms. Lawton, gave him a D on the project, despite his attempt to butter her up by repeating her name in the chorus and ending the song with: "We love you, Ms. Lawton, she's my favorite teacher ever," as Lil Timmy Tim and his female backup dancers made heart-hand signs to the camera.

The actor has likely never used statistics since, but the video 100 percent came back to haunt him when a blogger discovered it on Ms. Lawton's Vimeo page in 2017—and the two-minute masterpiece went viral for all the reasons stated above. Two years later, during an appearance on *The Graham Norton Show*, the real Timmy Tim turned every shade of red as the British host played it for millions of TV viewers in the UK. He seemed even more embarrassed to explain why Ms. Lawton gave him such a poor grade. "Some people presented parabolas [a plane curve used in mathematics] and things that were more appropriate for statistics . . . mine was not," conceded Timothée.

The following year, as COVID-19 robbed the Class of 2020 a traditional graduation ceremony, the LaGuardia alum appeared on the *Graduate Together* TV special to address the high school seniors—as well as one memorable teacher, Ms. Lawton. "Thank you for your valiant efforts to teach me the art of statistics."

MET GALA

The style icon received one of the industry's top honors when he was named cochair of the 2021 Met Gala alongside singer Billie Eilish, tennis star Naomi Osaka, and poet Amanda Gorman. Timothée's interpretation of the annual event's theme, "In America: A Lexicon of Fashion," was unique: a white satin tuxedo jacket with black lapels and white sweatpants by Haider Ackermann and eighty-five dollar Converse All-Star high-tops, all of which he tied together with a vintage 1920s Cartier brooch fastened at his waist. The monochromatic look was meant to counteract the "constant cacophony we exist in right now," Ackermann revealed to *Vogue*. "I wanted to keep everything in white—calm expression of hope and light."

Timothée looked like a work of art, literally. Shortly before the Met Gala red carpet, he took part in an installation nearby at the museum The Frick Collection, a collaboration between French street artist JR and composer Nicholas Britell. As a cinematographer's camera rolled, the actor sat contemplatively in a gallery. He then got up and tore through a black-and-white paper American flag, leading him to wander around The Frick. "We enter in an American flag, to find a place, an identity, a position, a future, between the stripes and the stars," JR explained to the fashion magazine. "To get to the end, we need to confront our rifts, our flaws, those of our nation, of our family, and our own cracks which have been amplified by two years of loneliness, anger, fear, confrontation."

Cameras continued to follow Timothée as he exited The Frick and walked several blocks north to The Metropolitan Museum of Art on Fifth Avenue—picking up fans along the way—and arriving at the Gala just in time to hit the red carpet.

NEW YORK KNICKS

Timothée may not look like your average diehard sports fan, but the native New Yorker bleeds blue and orange for his favorite NBA team, the Knicks. His passion dates back to childhood and was even documented in local newspapers in 2010 when the fourteen-year-old waited for hours to get an autograph from basketball star Amar'e Stoudemire, a free agent the Knicks were hoping to sign. As the article explained, Stoudemire was in New York and tweeted his plan to catch the musical *Rock of Ages*, so Timothée grabbed a Knicks jersey and booked it to the Brooks Atkinson Theatre on West Forty-Seventh Street—where paparazzi were already waiting.

Not only did the teen get Stoudemire's autograph on his way out of the show, but the moment was also captured by cameras. In the papers the next day, Timothée was quoted in *Newsday* recalling his brief conversation with Stoudemire: "He kinda nodded and said, 'What's good, man?'" In the sports section of the *New York Daily News*, however, he was cropped out of the photo, and, worse yet, his name was misspelled as "Tim Charamet." "He smiled at me," the teen said of Stoudemire. "That was reason enough to come down here. I think he is the answer for what the Knicks need."

Timothée was right: Stoudemire did end up signing with the team (and improved their record). But he was off on another Knicks prediction—and it proved costly. Amid rumors that LeBron James was headed to New York, Timothée spent his entire first paycheck from a Disney commercial on season tickets (albeit in the nosebleed section). The NBA superstar ultimately announced he was going to the Miami Heat, which meant Timothée spent many afternoons in front of Madison Square Garden trying to scalp his tickets. In a twist of fate, eight years later the Oscar-nominated actor was invited by the Knicks to sit courtside in "Celebrity Row" at a 2018 game. "They said, 'Hey, we're gonna throw you on the big screen,'" he recalled to *GQ*. "And I said, 'Please don't—you're gonna realize that nobody knows me, and you'll never have me back.'"

OFFICE OBSESSION

All throughout the filming of *Beautiful Boy*, Timothée was harboring a deep secret from his costar Steve Carell: he was completely obsessed with his NBC sitcom *The Office*. Why not tell him? "I think I didn't want to scare Steve away," he confessed to *IndieWire*. In fact, the fanboy didn't reveal it until the *Beautiful Boy* press tour. "Now I can be honest about it and a total weirdo."

Timothée was too young to get into *The Office*—which launched the careers of John Krasinski, Mindy Kaling, B. J. Novak, and Rainn Wilson—when it first premiered back in 2005. But when reruns began streaming on Netflix, the youngster figured out how to watch episodes through his Xbox Live, and it became a bonding activity with his father, Marc. "This was before the smart TVs and everything," Timothée told *IndieWire*. "My dad would be kind of amazed that on my video game console I could just pull up Netflix and all this streaming was available at the fingertips, which is true now, but I'm talking when I was thirteen, fourteen, fifteen . . . I'd get on my soccer beanbag chair, and he'd lie down next to me, and we'd put on *The Office*, and we'd watch like three, four episodes in a row, and not hit the skip theme song in the beginning, and watch it each time."

In the years since the series went off the air in 2013 after nine seasons, there's been hope among fans (and NBC) for a reboot. Timothée has said he "would love to" appear in an episode. But alas, "Steve is pretty clear that that's not a thing that is in their ambition."

PAULINE

The Chalamet family is full of talent—Timothée's sister, Pauline, is also an actress, who's appeared in HBO's *The Sex Lives of College Girls* and *The King of Staten Island* starring Pete Davidson. Although the siblings started on similar paths, both attending LaGuardia High School, Pauline, who is three years older, blazed her own trail. She went to college at Bard, a hundred miles north of Manhattan, and double-majored in theater and political science. To pay off her school loans, Pauline worked at the campus library and took a part-time weekend job on a farm. But she didn't immediately put her degree to use, bouncing around as a bartender and babysitter to make ends meet until she took off for Paris, where she enrolled in acting classes and rediscovered her passion. A writer and producer as well, Pauline cofounded Gummy Films and also appeared in the French television series *Split*.

"My sister's like my best friend today," Timothée told celeb interviewer Olivia Marks while promoting *Little Women*. But as a kid, she would torture him the only way an older sister could: she'd hide his shoes in places he couldn't reach and even changed her computer's desktop photo to a shot of her pulling Timothée's hair while they were on vacation in Italy. What's it like now that he's one of the world's most famous heartthrobs? Pauline, who gave birth to her first child in 2024, lives mostly in France, so "I don't really experience the frenzy around him," she told *W Magazine*. "Timothée is a hard worker. When I see him on the big screen, for me that's just the result of his job."

QUARTER-LIFE CRISIS

Timothée turned twenty-five in 2020, several months into the COVID-19 pandemic, and during his initial time in quarantine, "It required me to take a step back and be humbled," he admitted to British *Vogue*. At the time, he had several projects in the works, such as *Dune* and *A Complete Unknown*, that were indefinitely put on hold, sending him into an existential spiral. After two years as one of the most in-demand actors in Hollywood, everything suddenly halted, and he was overwhelmed with the very thought of taxes and dentist appointments. "I should have been trying to get my adult feet under myself a little bit earlier than I did," he fretted. "I found myself having to really, you know, be honest with myself that where I've been able to get myself to in life was balls to the wall, like throwing everything at [it] at a young age that, by some miracle, got me to where I am. But to then transition to an adulting mindset . . ."

Mentally climbing the walls in his Manhattan apartment, Timothée escaped to upstate New York to Woodstock, the bucolic town where Bob Dylan lived in the 1960s, and rented a cabin for the month of July. There he listened to music, played guitar and harmonica in peace, cooked "shitty pasta," and just gave in to the stillness of his life for the first time since the merry-go-round began in 2017—for better or worse. "I had spent a lot of time after high school with my head in the clouds, imagining a life as an actor, and totally oblivious to the life I was actually leading," Timothée recalled to *GQ* three years later as the time finally came to begin shooting *A Complete Unknown*. "I was *out of touch* with an *in-touch* life. And during COVID, it flipped, and I was forced to become very *in touch* with my increasingly *out-of-touch* life. It was not good for me."

REAL ESTATE

The native New Yorker headed west in 2022 when he purchased an $11 million estate in Beverly Hills. The four-bedroom, five-bathroom home—described in its real estate listing as "timeless East Coast"—is nestled in Benedict Canyon, hidden behind a private gated drive, with amenities spread across its 1.55 acres (0.62 ha), including a tennis court (put in by former owner, seven-time Wimbledon champ Pete Sampras), swimming pool, jacuzzi spa, and an entertainment area with a bar, wine cellar, and home theater.

Timothée bought the property "on a whim" from Houston Astros pitcher Justin Verlander and supermodel Kate Upton fewer than two weeks before he left to film *Dune: Part Two*. "During the throes of COVID it felt like people that were in LA with a little more privacy had it better figured out than I did," he confessed to *GQ*. Even just the little bit of time he got to spend at home before heading off to Budapest to film the sci-fi sequel "psychologically helped."

SATURDAY NIGHT LIVE

Everyone knows Timothée is a serious dramatic actor, but most people had yet to witness his comedic chops until he hosted *Saturday Night Live* for the first time in December 2020. As he revealed in his opening monologue, the show was inherent for the native New Yorker: his mother Nicole worked as an extra on *SNL*, which he showed in a clip from a "Massive Head Wound Harry" sketch starring Dana Carvey and Chris Farley from 1991—four years before Timothée was born.

His debut pulled in the second-highest ratings that season (behind comedian Dave Chappelle), thanks to a viral skit that transformed

Timothée into a pink-haired rapper named $mokeCheddaThaAssGetta. The character was so popular, he reprised the role for his second hosting gig in 2023 to promote the musical *Wonka*. Timothée gave viewers a glimpse of his singing skills in the opening monologue with a parody of the film's "Pure Imagination" about his own "world of shameless self-promotion." Later in the episode, his dance moves (and red underwear) were also on display in "Troye Sivan Sleep Demon," in which he portrayed the "gay famous" Australian pop star whose antics are causing sleep paralysis for Sarah Sherman.

TIMEPIECE COLLECTION

Timothée's watch collection is, well, timeless: the actor has amassed vintage pieces from Cartier, Rolex, and Jaeger-LeCoultre. As a longtime ambassador for Cartier, naturally he has several rare watches, including the luxury jeweler's "holy grail," the Cartier Crash—one of only 267 in existence. The $100,000 masterpiece's face is asymmetrically shaped (as if it's been in a literal crash) and adorned with 150 diamonds that dazzled on his wrist when Timothée wore it to the 2024 Golden Globes. He's also accessorized with the equally expensive Cartier Tank a Vis, which features a white-gold face, Roman numerals to tell the time, and a black leather band. The Cartier Tank is considered the world's first gender-neutral watch and has been worn by everyone from Princess Diana and Jackie Onassis to Muhammad Ali.

The first luxury timepiece that adorned Timothée's wrist is the Jaeger-LeCoultre Reverso, which was his mainstay throughout the 2018 award season (in both steel and rose gold). Moderately priced (comparatively) at approximately $7,000, the Art Deco–style relic was crafted nearly a century ago for polo players who didn't want to scratch their watches—a mechanism flips the face over for protection. For the 2020 Academy Awards, Timothée was so proud of his timepiece for the occasion, he tweeted it (in all caps, no less): "ROSE GOLD PRESIDENTIAL ON MY BONEY WRIST." Officially known as the Rolex Day-Date, the precious instrument earned its name because the chronometer displays the day of the week spelled out and the date. The president bracelet also has a royal feature: it's fitted with a concealed Rolex crown clasp for a "final aesthetic and functional touch."

ULTIMATE INSPIRATIONS

Timothée's Mount Rushmore of personal heroes is rock solid. The most significant influence is rapper-actor Kid Cudi, "My favorite artist ever," he gushed on *The Tonight Show Starring Jimmy Fallon* in 2019. "I wouldn't be acting without him; I wouldn't pursue this crazy career." They say don't meet your idols, but Timothée did just that in 2013 when he was introduced to Kid Cudi in Montreal, where the rapper had a concert. A mutual friend set it up, and the two "chilled" for hours, listening to music and talking about Timothée's concerns about the Hollywood industry. "Timothée says I'm responsible for his acting career and I'm like 'you're a crazy motherfucker for saying that,'" Cudi joked to *Esquire* in 2022.

Another musician who had a profound impact on Timothée is Frank Ocean, a two-time Grammy winner in the alternative R&B genre. In 2018, the two interviewed each other for *VMan* magazine, and Timothée had no chill the moment Ocean said hello. "This is so exciting. It is an honor to speak to you, man. I'm such a huge fan," he rambled. "This is going to be a real test to keep my voice level and keep this as normal of a conversation as possible." Timothée managed to keep it together, aside from busting out a line from Ocean's song "Raf" mid-interview when the singer mentioned fashion designer Raf Simons. "Thank you so much for this," he gushed at the end of the conversation. "It's been such an experience, sharing personal thoughts about artistry and acting with someone that's influenced me in many ways. This means the world to me."

His "number one" favorite actor is Academy Award–winner Joaquin Phoenix, especially his performance in 2012's *The Master*, for which he earned his third Best Actor nomination. Inspired by his genius, Timothée scoured Phoenix's interviews for any shred of advice, and one comment resonated. "He said he's not as interested in wearing different scarves inasmuch as he is in chasing a certain feeling. What that feeling is, he has no idea what it is, but he's chasing it," Timothée recalled to *The Playlist*. Seven years later, the two Hollywood heavyweights finally met at the 2024 Golden Globe Awards, where they were both up for Best Performance by a Male Actor in a Motion Picture—and both lost to Paul Giamatti. In photos, Timothée looks positively giddy as he chats with Phoenix.

He got the opportunity to work with his second-favorite actor, Leonardo DiCaprio, in 2021's *Don't Look Up*, an ensemble apocalyptic satire that featured Timothée in a small-but-memorable role as a shoplifting skateboarder who romances Jennifer Lawrence's character, an astronomer who discovers a comet is headed straight for Earth. In the film, the two link up with an astronomy professor played by DiCaprio, and it took every ounce of DiCaprio's acting ability not to break character and crack up at Timothée's improvised lines. "He was killing Leo," Lawrence recalled in a Netflix cast discussion. One scene in particular, the actress recalled DiCaprio's face growing redder as he held his breath trying not to laugh until the cameras cut. "He would say the most random stuff, but it was incredible," revealed DiCaprio.

VOGUE

"The most influential man in fashion," Timothée was celebrated accordingly in October 2022 as the first solo male on the cover of British *Vogue* in the magazine's 106-year history. Shot by legendary fashion photographer Steven Meisel, the edgy *Bones and All*–inspired pictorial is equally gender-bending with the actor styled in womenswear pieces like a Stella McCartney chain-mail top, Miu Miu leather boots, and a pearl necklace. "The beauty of the shoot. It wasn't male, it wasn't female," British *Vogue* editor-in-chief Edward Enninful told Timothée in an accompanying video interview. The decision to make him the fashion bible's first male cover model "was a no-brainer," added Enninful. "I was like, 'Who is it? Who sort of represents now? Who is sort of loved by people of all ages?' Somebody who was so first, and great at the idea of imagery and translating characters—and it was you."

WONKA DUNKS

Forget golden tickets, to promote *Wonka* the film's star gave away five pairs of limited-edition Nike Dunk Lows inspired by the iconic candymaker. Timothée traveled to the brand's campus in Beaverton, Oregon, to custom-design the shoes in the spirit of his character: chocolate brown outsole; scribbles of purple, burgundy, and light blue (from the pattern of his character's coat's inner lining) on the white canvas base; burgundy velvet (the coat's material) for the Nike swoosh, tongue, and laces; and a chocolate brown tongue tag with a golden "W" completed the Wonka Dunk, which was packaged in a burgundy velvet shoe bag and placed inside a wooden box.

"Visiting Beaverton was like visiting the real Willy Wonka Factory," Timothée, an admitted sneakerhead, told *Complex*. "So, to get to partner with them under the guise of a chocolatier, I just knew how lucky I was. I was a kid in a candy store." A total of eight pairs were produced, including one for Timothée and another for his *Dune* costar Zendaya "because she's awesome." The five contest winners were selected for their one-minute submission videos showcasing how *Wonka* inspires their own creativity. Robin Wray of Guilford, Indiana, was one of the lucky recipients—chosen for her wonderfully whimsical candy-themed Christmas tree. "I've been bombarded by sneaker collectors from around the globe asking me 'How much for the Wonka Dunks?'" she told local news outlet *The 812*. "My answer is, they're not for sale."

XBOX 360

Timothée's double life as a gamer is not so surprising, but his secret past as an Xbox 360 influencer came as a shock when his YouTube channel was discovered in 2021. As a youngster, he had a knack for specially modifying controllers—and he showed off his latest creations as @ModdedController360. Although it would be many years before he became famous, Timothée still wanted to keep his identity under wraps, so he filmed each video from the neck down, in his bedroom at home.

"What's good, YouTube?" he greeted followers in the first clip, the debut of a Christmas-themed "modded controller" done in red and green. "It works perfectly," he noted, demonstrating how all the buttons were unaffected by the spray paint. In his second video, Timothée proudly showed a silver-and-blue controller and asked followers to leave comments telling him what color combos to try next. The third and final installment was all about a red-and-black striped controller he was selling for ten dollars. "It looks nice, it looks sexy," he told viewers.

When the long-dormant @ModdedController360 channel resurfaced, *Vice* launched an investigation to confirm the mysterious gamer was indeed a young Timothée. The team spent weeks analyzing evidence, like photos of his hands and childhood bedroom, only for the *Dune* actor to beat them to it, announcing his secret past in an interview with *Inside Edition*. Timothée embraced his alter ego at the 2023 Games Awards, where he was introduced as "Modded Controller 360" to present the award for Game of the Year to *Baldur's Gate 3*.

YOUNGARTS

Timothée's Hollywood achievements come as no surprise to those who recognized his talent long before he stepped on a film set. In 2013, the seventeen-year-old actor was selected from a pool of ten thousand applicants by the National YoungArts Foundation to participate in a weeklong workshop intended to develop his craft with internationally recognized leaders in theater. At the time, the young actor was coming off an eight-episode arc on *Homeland*. At YoungArts, "you don't have to worry about making a great form of entertainment," he said in a video on their YouTube channel. "You're just worrying about making great art and connecting with yourself again." Sure enough, that year he booked *Interstellar*.

YoungArts is the only organization in the US to recognize students in ten discipline categories: cinematic arts, dance, jazz, music, photography, theater, visual arts, voice, writing, and architecture. Timothée is one of Hollywood's noted YoungArts alumni that include Emmy Award–winning *Scandal* star Kerry Washington, EGOT (Emmy, Grammy, Oscar, Tony) winner Viola Davis, and Nicki Minaj, the best-selling female rapper in the world.

ZENDAYA

Timothée only got to spend five days with his *Dune* costar on set in 2019, but in that short span of time he and Zendaya forged a tight bond that didn't evaporate in the desert once filming wrapped. All throughout the 2021 press tour, the giggly pair were inseparable, inspiring BuzzFeed to give them a "BFF test." They passed with flying colors, as both knew each other's birthdays, middle names, favorite swear words, and Timothée even dished on Zendaya's "celebrity crush": her boyfriend, *Spider-Man* star Tom Holland. The actress got her revenge by revealing she once organized Timothée's New York apartment because she was shocked by its state. "This is like bachelor pad, guys," she emphasized as his face turned every shade of red. Three years later while promoting the *Dune* sequel on *Jimmy Kimmel Live!*, Zendaya detailed how she helped Timothée transform the space with a trip to Bed Bath & Beyond. "We just needed a few necessities—you know, cups and plates, knives and forks, things to clean . . . We got everything he needed, all the big boy stuff."

But in all seriousness, neither take for granted they get to have such a genuinely close relationship in Hollywood. "Zendaya is a friend for life," Timothée said on ABC's *Good Morning America*, "and I'm counting my lucky stars that I've got a friend in this crazy industry that I can count on, and she's got the same here." Zendaya felt the love, gushing to *People*, "I'm just so grateful that this experience has been with this guy because he's massively talented but also such a good person."

"THE SCARIEST YEAR"

In 2014, after two semesters at Columbia University, Timothée made the agonizing decision to drop out of school—against his parents' wishes—and pursue acting full-time. *Interstellar* was set to arrive in theaters that fall, and the eighteen-year-old was convinced that Christopher Nolan's epic space drama would launch his own career. "Nope," he admitted with a laugh to Emma Stone in a *Variety* Actors on Actors conversation. "I was very presumptuous." Over the next year, Timothée kept busy with a handful of roles, albeit in productions that were either panned by critics (*The Adderall Diaries, Love the Coopers*) or were so indie few people even saw it (*Miss Stevens*). "That was the scariest year of my life because I didn't have a career. I had tasted enough of this stuff where I kind of could see what it maybe could be, but it wasn't presenting itself." So in the fall of 2015, Timothée enrolled at New York University's Gallatin School of Individualized Study, which allowed him to take time off for film projects. He stuck with the program until 2018—when he was nominated for an Academy Award.

PART FOUR

Hollywood "It" Boy

MODERN MOVIE STAR

Timothée Chalamet has been compared to iconic Hollywood actors James Dean, Marlon Brando, Daniel Day-Lewis, and Leonardo DiCaprio. But Gen Z's leading man isn't a modern-day repeat—he's his own unique talent who has achieved global fame not just for his acclaimed films, but more so, his authenticity. Whether he's portraying a medieval king, a drug addict, or a kooky candymaker, Timothée digs deep into the raw emotions such as vulnerability, sensitivity, anxiety, and insecurity while others would prefer to stifle. His objective is to be an "open wound" capable of connecting with a wider audience through the screen. "I feel like I'm here to show that to wear your heart on your sleeve is OK," he explained to *Time* in 2021.

But most fans agree his impact is far more significant than just that. Timothée is "redefining masculinity, redefining what it is to be a leading male in a way that I think is very important for us right now," *Little Women* director Greta Gerwig explained to *Out*, an LGBTQ+ magazine that crowned the *Call Me by Your Name* actor "the straight prince of twinks." He was flattered and embraced the "good fortune" to portray a queer character in a film that "could present a version of love that people don't understand . . . that isn't prosecuted or persecuted, that it's just a thing."

It's a topic that Timothée has discussed with singer Harry Styles, whose androgynous style landed him on the cover of *Vogue* in 2020. In a conversation about "modern masculinity" for *i-D* magazine, the two icons shared their experiences pushing gender-normative boundaries in their respective industries. "Today it's easier to embrace masculinity in so many different things," noted Harry. "I definitely find—through music, writing, talking with friends, and being open—that some of the times when I feel most confident is when I'm allowing myself to be vulnerable." Timmy concurred, "It's almost a high to be vulnerable," especially when portraying a character who could initiate change. "It's a brave new world. Maybe it's because of social media, maybe it's because of who the fuck knows what, but there's a real excitement from our generation about doing things in a new way."

CREATIVE LICENSE

Looking at Timothée's filmography, you'd be hard-pressed to find even one mediocre performance. He's allowed himself the freedom to choose projects based on their significance and works exclusively with extraordinary directors, regardless of whether it's the lead role or a minor

"There's a real excitement from our generation about doing things in a new way."

character. "I guess I'm trying to go where it's not obvious to go," he told British *Vogue* in 2022, as he tackled his most unexpected to date, the musical *Wonka*. "To work on something that will have an uncynical young audience, that was just a big joy. That's why I was drawn to it. In a time and climate of intense political rhetoric, when there's so much bad news all the time, this is hopefully going to be a piece of chocolate."

Timothée took even more control over his storytelling as a producer, beginning with *Bones and All*. The star of the film was integral in the collaborative process, working with director Luca Guadagnino to secure financing—not an easy feat for a cannibal love story—as well as screenwriter David Kajganich to retool his character. By making Lee as fragile as his love interest, Maren (Russell Taylor), they could show his emotional journey when "someone you're in love with breaks you down,"

Timothée explained to *IndieWire*. "That's where I feel I earned my producer credit on this. I hope all my input was warranted. You never want to get to a place where people take your input because they have to and actually all your ideas are terrible."

Proving that he has the right instincts, Warner Bros. signed Timothée to a multiyear deal in 2024, allowing him to collaborate with the studio—which distributed *Dune* and *Wonka*—on films as both an actor and a producer. "We have admired not only Timothée's commitment to his craft, which is evident in the range and depth of his varied roles, but also his unwavering dedication to give a hundred percent of his time and attention to every project he has made here at Warner Bros. and elsewhere," studio CEOs Mike De Luca and Pam Abdy said in a joint statement. Timothée praised the pair for their belief "in real movie making, and I'm so grateful for their support as an actor, producer and collaborator. This partnership feels like a natural next step. Let's go!"

LEARNING FROM THE GREATS

Timothée's filmography reads like a who's who of Hollywood heavyweights. He's shared the screen with Academy Award–winners Meryl Streep, Leonardo DiCaprio, Laura Dern, Olivia Colman, Frances McDormand, and Javier Bardem. Of his own generation, countless more costars have already racked up several Oscar nominations, representing the new wave of talent, such as Saoirse Ronan, Florence Pugh, and Austin Butler. And from each person he's taken something invaluable, whether it's advice (DiCaprio famously told him, "No hard drugs or superhero movies") or simply just watching them work. "I love being able to see how people sink into the material—like watching you work your way through scenes, trying new things, always keeping it fresh," Timothée told his first high-profile costar, *Interstellar*'s Matthew McConaughey, in *Interview* magazine. "Younger actors feel pressure to bring a pop to every scene. As the roles get bigger, I'm finding you can add layers and do less scene-to-scene."

There's still plenty to learn from those still in the ascension of their promising careers. Timothée was floored when he logged onto Zoom for a *Dune: Part Two* cast reading and Butler, who plays the nephew of Baron Harkonnen (Stellan Skarsgård), "was already *talking* like Stellan Skarsgård," Timothée told *GQ*. "I can't overstate how inspiring it was to me personally." Butler famously hung onto his Elvis Presley voice after starring in Baz Luhrmann's 2022 biopic, and now he had seamlessly moved on to Skarsgård. On the *Dune* set, Butler's dedication to his character made Timothée work even harder to rise to the same standard, said producer Cale Boyter. "I think any great actor has a competitiveness to them, and Timmy is no exception."

HEARTTHROB TO ART-THROB

Timothée has redefined the idea of a Hollywood leading man, inside and out—and from head to toe. On the red carpet, he shows his vulnerability in pinks and florals, revealing sleeveless shirts, pearl necklaces, and vintage brooches. Haider Ackermann, who has designed some of his most daring fashion statements, says they both see clothing as an artistic medium similar to acting. "The exchanges we share, the conversations, the mutual respect, and brotherhood permits us to operate in a vast playing field," Ackermann told *Vogue*. "This freedom has enabled us to constantly challenge the traditional ideals of masculinity. Timothée's courage and fearlessness in his beliefs makes him a writer of a new generation."

On the big screen, his innate sensitivities take center stage in every character he portrays. Timothée can easily move an audience to tears, whether he's playing a hopeless drug addict (*Beautiful Boy*) or a hopeless romantic (*Little Women*). In recent years, there's been a changing of the guard in Hollywood, as the era of the brooding tough guy exits stage left. "Today's leading man is a more sensitive, thoughtful person," talent agent David Unger told *New York Magazine*. "Timothée Chalamet exhibits a version of that. He's symbolic of the emotional young man."

And he's struck a chord with millions of fans around the world, as well as his equally enamored costars. *The King*'s Ben Mendelsohn witnessed the Chalamania firsthand during the film's press tour. "He's a fucking movie star," Mendelsohn told *Digital Spy*. "He's a better movie star than we deserve to have. I believe that. I really believe that. I've never heard a crowd scream louder for anyone in my life. I've been around some pretty fancy-pants people in my life. I've never heard people scream for a person the way they scream for Timothée. And Timmy touches people in a way that's quite profound."

END OF A GENERATIONAL CURSE

With Timothée leading the next generation of Hollywood actors, the future of cinema seems limitless. Even more exciting is the fact his equally talented colleagues all want to work with him again and again, from Zendaya (*Dune* franchise) and Greta Gerwig (*Lady Bird*, *Little Women*) to frequent costar Saoirse Ronan who actually would like to eventually move to the other side of the camera. "I'd act in a movie you directed in three seconds," Timothée told her during a joint *New York Times* interview in 2018. "I feel very lucky to have an older sister who always pointed out the

"I am learning that a good role isn't the only criteria for accepting a job."

dynamics of what it's like when a woman shares her ideas, how they're received compared to men's ideas. And being young, hopefully getting to act for years on end, changing that is our responsibility now—and our good fortune."

Timothée acknowledged that it's part of the job as an actor "to be more aware of the choices we're making," and he learned that lesson the hard way when he led the all-star cast of Woody Allen's *A Rainy Day in New York*. Shot in 2017, by the time the rom-com was in postproduction, past allegations of sexual abuse against the controversial director resurfaced amid the Me Too movement, and Amazon dropped the "unmarketable" film. "It's going to be important for me to talk about working with Woody," admitted Timothée to the *New York Times*. He let his actions do the speaking.

Timothée donated his salary from the film to several charities, including the Rape, Abuse & Incest National Network (RAINN), Time's Up, and the Lesbian, Gay, Bisexual & Transgender Community Center of New York. "I don't want to profit from my work on the film," he said in a statement. "I am learning that a good role isn't the only criteria for accepting a job."

THE INTERNET'S BOYFRIEND

For every article proclaiming "Timothée Chalamet Is Hollywood's Next Big Thing" (*The Los Angeles Times*), there's another asking "Why Is Everyone Obsessed with Timothée Chalamet?" (*The Telegraph*). The answer is as nuanced as how the heartthrob manages his foppish curls. As the French would say, he has that "Je ne sais quoi" (I don't know what)—an unexplainable appealing quality that has captivated millions of Chalamaniacs around the world. And he's done it by simply being himself, someone who is genuinely excited, charmingly awkward, self-deprecating yet sensitive, quirky, polite, thoughtful, hyperaware (and sometimes, just hyper).

"NO, I'M KIDDING."

Don't let the dramatic actor fool you—Timothée's comedic side is pretty much his whole offscreen persona. Sometimes, it's unintentional. In interviews especially, his nervous energy creates awkward hilarity, as he stammers, laughs at everything, fidgets in his chair, and rambles (abruptly stopping himself eventually). Early in his career, Timothée had such a penchant for following up an offhand remark with "No, I'm kidding!" that someone made a supercut of every single one, which has amassed over a million views on YouTube. It's just one of countless videos dedicated to the actor's signature quirk. Simply search "Timothée Chalamet awkward" and sit back and enjoy compilations like "Timothée Chalamet Being Awkward for 6 Minutes Straight."

At a 2019 panel about *The King*, Timothée was simply asked what attracted him to the film, and for two minutes he mentioned everything: toxic masculinity, Laurence Olivier, well-oiled machines, Brad Pitt, and an "Australian creative circus that travels" before wrapping it up. "I'll be quiet," he said, as the audience laughed. "I'm the youngest one here, people don't want to hear me." In an MTV interview to promote *Little Women*, Timothée gushed about his "awesome older sister" and then gestured up like she was in heaven, "but that doesn't make any sense," he laughed.

And it's not just fans who have noticed Timmy's adorably awkward moments. Harry Styles even brought it up during a joint interview for *i-D* magazine. "Sometimes on TV shows you can seem really nervous, but on screen you're an extremely confident actor," noted the singer. Timothée explained he wants to avoid "self-assumption" in social settings, "and I think that's what makes me nervous on talk shows . . . so I put myself in the

"Well, you're in the big time now,"
Hanks joked. "Get used to it."

audiences' shoes and imagine them seeing this young unrecognizable guy trying to talk about movies seriously."

Over the years, Timmy has eased into the spotlight, yet he hasn't lost his humility. During an appearance on *The Graham Norton Show* in 2023, he shared the couch with Tom Hanks, Julia Roberts, and Cher, when the topic turned to his upcoming portrayal of Bob Dylan, and it was revealed that Cher knew the folk singer back in the 1960s. Timothée's mind was blown. "This whole talk show has been, like, a trip," he marveled. "Well, you're in the big time now," Hanks joked. "Get used to it."

TIMMY & THE CHALAMANIACS

Fans are a big reason for Timothée's success. They watch his movies, tune in to award shows to see if he'll win, anticipate each red-carpet fashion

"All his questions were super sincere and genuine."

moment, and read every interview. Their support is not lost on him, and Timmy takes any opportunity to show his appreciation. At film premieres, he signs autographs, poses for selfies, gives hugs, and even kisses on the cheek if you're really lucky. During these interactions, he's so genuinely engaged that he can recognize a familiar face. "I've seen you a couple times," he said, pointing to a fan in the audience at a 2018 BAFTA Guru panel in London. At the Venice Film Festival in 2019, Timothée did a double take as he leaned in to take a photo with a fan. "I've seen you before," he remarked—and sure enough, she reminded him where they had previously met. Another time, while walking the streets of Paris, a young fan stopped him to give him a book she made about his movies. "Wow, wow," Timmy repeated as he flipped through it and chatted with her in French.

One lucky young woman from India named Alankrutha got the one-in-a-zillion opportunity to sit next to Timothée on a three-hour flight—in economy, no less—and she detailed the experience in a 2019 viral X thread. Alankrutha asked Timmy hard-hitting questions like "Have you met Beyoncé?" and the two gabbed about their shared love of *The Office*. "What shocks me the most is this dude wanted to know about me," she gushed. "He asked me what I do, what project management is about (literally who cares, Timothée), where I grew up and PRONOUNCED MY NAME RIGHT . . . And all his questions were super sincere and genuine." When they landed, Timmy asked her to take a selfie and "wished me luck for my career."

VIRAL SENSATION

Timothée could read the phonebook and it would go viral. After all, one of his earliest internet-breaking moments was the discovery of his rap persona, Lil Timmy Tim. At the 2018 SAG Awards—where he was nominated for Outstanding Performance by a Male Actor in a Leading Role—he waxed poetic about Cardi B on the red carpet and sang "Bartier Cardi" in his *Access Hollywood* interview. The following year at the awards show, cameras panned the audience and stopped momentarily on Emily Blunt and John Krasinki's table, but all anyone at home focused on was Timothée in the background engrossed in what looked like a book. On X, the topic trended throughout the remainder of the broadcast: what was Timmy reading? No, it wasn't an SAT book, as widely guessed. In typical Timmy fashion, it was the award ceremony's oversized program. Another unintentionally viral moment was at the 2024 *Dune: Part Two* premiere, when Timothée can be seen awkwardly greeting Anya Taylor-Joy, then whispering something to Zendaya. Lip-reader-extraordinaire @TisMeJackieG, a deaf content creator with a half-million followers, decoded what a dejected-looking Timmy said to Z: "I'm not ok."

All over YouTube and TikTok, one of his most embarrassing moments lives on: Timothée laughing so hard he fell backward out of his chair at a Q&A event for *Call Me by Your Name*. "This is so embarrassing," he said as the audience howled. "How am I going to recover from this?" The internet refused to let him, but it was worse for Timmy in the moment. "There was a girl in the audience that night I was super psyched was there, and then that happened," he said on *The Tonight Show Starring Jimmy Fallon*—before throwing himself out the chair, this time on purpose. In his most popular video on YouTube, Timothée actually saves someone else from embarrassment. At a *Little Women* photocall in London, he was posing with Saoirse Ronan when the strap slipped on her dress, which he artfully blocked from the cameras by stepping in front of her and pretending to be in conversation. Uploaded in 2022, the nine-second video clip has 134 million views.

Timmy has reached a new level of fame where anyone who even looks like him can go viral. In 2023, ChaChou Miyake-Mugler, a thin-framed ballroom dancer with Timmy's same poofy hair, was christened Chala-Slay after a video of him voguing in a catsuit and thigh-high boots hit the web. The real Timothée was in the middle of *Wonka* promotion when Heart FM's Dev Griffin showed him the video everyone was talking about. The actor watched in disbelief, both at the uncanny resemblance and Chala-Slay's moves. "That was insane," he raved. "I'm gonna watch that again on my own time."

HE'S A FANBOY, TOO!

It doesn't matter how famous Timmy is, he's just like the rest of us when he meets a celebrity he has long admired. In 2017, he costarred with Christian Bale in *Hostiles*, and "I remember him asking me to repeat my name so he could hear it better," Timmy recounted to *Time Out*, "[but] my voice got caught in my throat." When he worked with Steve Carell in *Beautiful Boy*, *The Office* superfan decided to keep it to himself because "I didn't want to scare Steve away," he told *IndieWire*. Doubling his excitement, also in the film is Amy Ryan, who played Carell's onscreen wife on the NBC sitcom that ended in 2013. Timmy overheard the two discussing if a new generation had tapped into *The Office*, "and I'm, like, pulling my hair out of my head." In *Little Women*, he got to share the screen with his *Harry Potter* crush, Emma Watson—however, the first time they met was in an "icebreaker" dance class. Timmy felt so awkward, he joked to *Late Night* host Seth Meyers that he needed "tons of therapy" to move past the embarrassment.

BEST DRESSED

Timothée's style is as bold as his film repertoire: a redefined masculinity that artfully pushes boundaries. On red carpets from Hollywood to Cannes, the actor has all eyes on him, whether he's wearing a bespoke suit or a backless halter top. He brings the same energy to his street style, an effortless mix of high- and low-end items like Celine jackets and Chanel hoodies with Converse sneakers. "Fashion has always been so fun to me," Timmy told British *Vogue* in 2023. "I've always loved the idea that you can appropriately express yourself through clothes."

As a teen in New York City, Timothée wasn't afraid to experiment with his style. "Honestly, it was the women's clothes at Topshop for me," he admitted to *Vogue*. "That's the stuff that just fit growing up." As one of Hollywood's most promising young talents, his options expanded as he got the opportunity to work with some of his favorite designers, such as Haider Ackermann, Raf Simons, Yves Saint Laurent creative director Hedi Slimane, and the late Virgil Abloh of Off-White. "These guys are like rock stars," Timothée raved to *VMan*. "They're artists."

And he is their muse. Ackermann exclusively dressed Timothée for the defining moment of his young career, as a Best Actor nominee at the 2018 Academy Awards. To stand out among the veteran competition more than twice his age, Ackermann put Timothée in an all-white suit. "I wanted him to be pure," the French designer told *GQ*. Simons, then creative director of Calvin Klein, went the opposite route at that year's SAG (Screen Actors Guild) Awards, creating a black-on-black tuxedo and satin tie for the Outstanding Performance by a Male Actor nominee. Timothée may have lost to Gary Oldman at both awards shows, but he arguably won on the red carpet.

Ever since, every major promo tour has been a parade of Prada, Louis Vuitton, Gucci, Givenchy, Alexander McQueen, and Tom Ford, as Timothée raises the bar higher and higher for Hollywood. Here are five of his blockbuster moments in fashion.

HARNESSING HIS SELF-EXPRESSION

Fashionistas agreed the Best Supporting Performance nominee at the 2019 Golden Globes stylishly pushed the envelope with a black sequined harness-type accessory, worn over a black collarless tuxedo shirt and black trousers, all designed by Louis Vuitton's menswear artistic director Virgil Abloh. On the red carpet, reporters weren't quite sure what to make of the item that was also referred to as a half-vest. Timmy set the record straight: it was a "bib" originally meant to be worn under a suit. But hours before the awards ceremony, when he tried it on with the jacket, he called Abloh on FaceTime for his expert opinion. "He said, 'Nah, go without it . . . that's the way it's presenting itself,'" Timmy recounted to *Entertainment Tonight*. "That's all it was, you know, it's a form of artistic expression." He sheepishly admitted he was surprised to learn that some perceived the "harness" to be associated with "sex dungeon culture."

SUSTAINABLE FASHION

Timmy is no stranger to a bold pattern, and at the London photocall for *Dune* in 2021, he stepped out in his most adventurous outfit to date: mushrooms. Stella McCartney custom-made the actor a blue-and-ivory seersucker suit printed in her whimsical Fungi Forest toile—a fabric partially made from "zero-deforestation viscose"—which the designer had debuted weeks earlier on the runway of her Spring/Summer 2022 collection. "Every year, 150 million trees are cut down to create viscose," McCartney explained in *Elle* India, so she's committed to sourcing her material from "sustainably managed and certified forests in Sweden." Timmy is quite conscious of his fashion footprint: in addition to wearing McCartney's tailored suits and recycled jeans, he also experimented with Prada's Re-Nylon range (made from discarded plastic waste) at the 2020 Academy Awards and arrived at the Venice International Film Festival that same year carrying an eco-friendly Loewe messenger bag crafted from recycled, organic polyester.

BACKBONE AND ALL

It's not unusual for Timmy to go shirtless on the red carpet, but at the 2022 Venice International Film Festival to premiere *Bones and All*, he went backless and sleeveless in a shimmery red halter jumpsuit custom-designed by Haider Ackermann, with input from the actor. "We wanted to create a moment and raise questions, to see how far we could go with something, to see what could be done with a man who is very masculine showing his sensibility, showing his nudity," Ackermann revealed to *Vogue*. "I noticed the assurance he had when he started walking and looking at himself in the mirror, and I was like, OK, we have to do something challenging as you feel so confident and you look at yourself with such self-assurance." It was a bold statement—and most people liked what Timmy had to say. The red halter with a scarf-like neckline lit up social media. On X, one fan wrote, "timothée chalamet [sic] woke up and decided to end us all." *Vanity Fair* was a bit more poetic in its praise: "Timothée Chalamet Causes Transoceanic Commotion With Backless Outfit in Venice."

CANDY MAN

In November 2023, Timmy sweetened the London premiere of *Wonka* in a magenta velvet suit by Tom Ford, fresh off the runway at Milan Fashion Week. Perhaps even more daring was the actor's choice to go shirtless beneath his blazer, despite the near-freezing temperatures. "It's a nice chilly night," he remarked to fans on the red carpet, as the icy breeze from the nearby River Thames hit his bare chest. "I don't know what the hell I was doing wearing this." On the plus side, the suit's deep V-neck showed off his one-of-a-kind accessory: a Cartier necklace made of 964 pink tourmalines, emeralds, rubellites, and blue opals fitted to the contour of his throat. Timmy, an ambassador for the jeweler, helped to design the dazzling custom piece that required 450 hours to make. "It's beyond anything I could have dreamt," he told British *Vogue* of the necklace, which ultimately joined The Cartier Collection's traveling exhibit around the world.

TWINNING WITH TIMMY

What happens when Hollywood's two most stylish people star in the same film? Well, they hit the red carpet in the same ensemble. It was a coordinated effort between Timmy and Zendaya, who rocked matching leather jumpsuits—his in gray; hers in pink—by South Korean designer Juun.J for the Seoul promotion of *Dune: Part Two* in 2024. What set the duo apart is how they each styled the piece: Zendaya cinched the belt high and unzipped the jumpsuit so it fell off one shoulder, while Timmy wore it baggier, paired with pastel gray boots (and two silver Cartier necklaces). The fashion moment was made possible by Zendaya's "image architect" Law Roach, who typically opts for archival vintage pieces for his A-list client. "I think it's wonderful to support the designers here," Timmy said in a clip posted by *Vogue* Korea on Instagram. "This was Law's beautiful idea and creation. But thank you to Juun.J for this opportunity to wear his beautiful clothes."

EVERYONE'S FAVORITE COSTAR

In a town of make believe, Timothée Chalamet is a real one. With each film project, he's made genuine connections, turning costars and even directors into friends he hopes to keep for a lifetime. And they feel the same. "He's obviously a very talented actor, but just a wonderful person and a good friend to have," Zendaya revealed to British *Vogue* in 2021 about her *Dune* love interest. "Especially in this industry, it's nice to have other people who are going through it too and that you can talk to."

MATTHEW MCCONAUGHEY

Timmy's been charming cast members since his very first film set of Christopher Nolan's *Interstellar* in 2013. Although he had a relatively small part as the son of McConaughey's character, the newbie left a lasting impression on the Oscar winner. After shooting their shared scenes in Canada, the teen returned to New York to begin his freshman year at Columbia University—yet remained on McConaughey's mind as he continued filming the sci-fi drama set in outer space. In fact, after a heartbreaking scene in which his character watches video messages from his children back on earth, he picked up the phone to tell Timmy "I thought about you" in a voicemail that meant so much to the young actor he committed it to memory. Years later, his "movie dad" was as proud as his real one when Timmy was nominated for Best Actor at the 2018 Academy Awards. "He's a good young man," McConaughey boasted to ABC on the red carpet. "He's here to stay."

KIERNAN SHIPKA

Two years before Timothée broke out in *Call Me by Your Name*, he got to share the screen with the *Mad Men* actress, playing her brother in the 2015 indie thriller *One & Two*. The sibling bond translated off-screen, as Shipka's mother and father also treated Timothée like a son. When he was auditioning for *Beautiful Boy*, the New Yorker spent several months in Los Angeles and often crashed with the family, who "really made me feel like one of their own," Timothée told *W Magazine*. "Her mom drove me to that last call back with Steve Carell." Like a true big brother, he even chaperoned the sixteen-year-old actress on a date once. "It was a lunch with a boy," Shipka recalled on *Late Night with Seth Meyers* in 2022, "and I

*"I always knew
he was very special."*

didn't necessarily know what the vibe was yet so I wanted to bring a friend. And Timmy was the only person around, so I brought him."

SAOIRSE RONAN
Another longtime Hollywood confidante is his costar from *Lady Bird* and *Little Women*, whose natural rapport with Timothée translates to the big screen whether they're playing romantic interests (Lady Bird and Kyle) or best friends in love (Jo and Laurie). Ronan took the newbie under her wing on the set of Greta Gerwig's coming-of-age film and made it a point to invite Timothée along for after-work cocktails with the crew—except he was only twenty. "She goes, 'Oh, you don't have a fake ID?'" he recalled in an interview with ABC News. Timothée made an awkward joke "and she walked away, and I kind of wanted to go, 'No! Come back!' Like, 'Please think I'm cool!'" Ronan thinks he's much more than that. "I always knew he was very special," she told *Dazed* in 2020. "He's someone who I want to

"He's literally my favorite person."

continue to work with because I'm just quite interested to see how it goes. As we get older and when we have more and more experience—what it's like when we come back together."

FLORENCE PUGH

Friends to lovers—on the big screen: Timothée and Pugh have costarred in two films, *Little Women* and *Dune: Part Two*, and both times their characters got married. And as it turned out, she wasn't exactly his first choice either instance. But there are no hard feelings for the English actress, who had to be separated from Timothée on the *Dune* set "because they were having too much fun," director Denis Villeneuve told *Time*. The duo is so dynamic, it's left some wondering if perhaps their onscreen chemistry is art imitating life. Fans clued in on their flirtations throughout *Dune*'s promotion in

2024. In an interview with *Vogue*, Pugh couldn't remember the first time she met Timothée, who turned to the camera and remarked "the whole story's not appropriate." Zendaya, sitting between the two, raised an eyebrow. "What happened?" she asked. Neither would say, only to tease the evening in question "was really lovely and friendly."

SELENA GOMEZ

When photos emerged of Timothée and the actress-singer kissing in 2017, the internet nearly combusted. But it was a false alarm: the two hotties were shooting Woody Allen's rom-com *A Rainy Day in New York*. Timothée and Gomez stayed close, and teased fans over the years with Instagram Live appearances. "He's literally my favorite person," Gomez told fans in a 2017 stream. Three years later, they joined virtual forces again to encourage people to vote in the 2020 election. The friendship took an interesting turn when Timothée brought his girlfriend Kylie Jenner to the 2024 Golden Globes. Gomez was also there with Taylor Swift and a video of the two whispering to each other went viral as armchair lip-readers speculated the actress had said Jenner wouldn't allow Timothée to take a photo with her. Gomez denied the rumor and Timothée also confirmed there was no bad blood when TMZ caught up to him, answering "of course" when asked if he and Gomez were still cool.

AUSTIN BUTLER

It was a true bromance on the set of *Dune: Part Two*. Although Timothée and Butler played enemies from the warring Houses Atreides and Harkonnen, respectively, it was just some really great acting—because the two liked each other a lot. Before arriving on set in Hungary to rehearse their epic battle sequence, Timothée and Butler (who have mutual friends) had not yet met face-to-face, only ever interacting over Zoom for virtual table reads of the script. "I did feel that there were some sparks between both actors," Villeneuve revealed to the *Los Angeles Times*. Their fight-to-the-death scene left both actors battered and bruised, but still good buddies. "Timmy, he's a good friend now. I love him," Butler gushed to Dolby at the film's New York premiere. "What a legend he is." His character Feyd-Rautha—spoiler alert!—did not survive the sequel, but the two hope to work together again, and Timothée even has a dream collaboration in mind: a "musical cinematic universe" featuring his Bob Dylan from *A Complete Unknown* and Butler's Elvis Presley.

PETE DAVIDSON

Even before Timothée hosted *Saturday Night Live* in 2020, he was pals with one of the show's funniest stars. In January 2019, the two New Yorkers attended a private birthday dinner in Malibu for their mutual friend, rapper Kid Cudi, with Kanye West and Kim Kardashian (Davidson's future girlfriend). The following year, Timothée made his *SNL* debut and he and Davidson partnered on several hilarious sketches, including "Rap Roundtable" featuring the two as tattooed rap duo $mokeCheddaThaAssGetta and Guaplord who contributed mostly unintelligible commentary ("Yeet! Skrt!") during a serious discussion with Queen Latifah (played by Punkie Johnson) and Questlove from The Roots. "It's annoying because he's really attractive and talented," Davidson told *Gold Derby* in 2021. "Usually you're only allowed one, like I am . . . He's just one of those people that you're like, 'What the fuck is up with this kid?' Then you meet him and you're like, 'Oh yeah, I get it. Charming, nice, talented—Okay I get it.'"

TERMS OF ENDEARMENT

The French spelling of "Timothy," Timothée is pronounced Tim-oh-teh, "but I can't ask people to call me that; it just seems really pretentious," he joked to pal Frank Ocean in *VMan* magazine. As a kid, he went by Timmy and also tried out Tim and Timo, neither of which stuck. Now as an adult, several of his famous friends have christened him with their own nicknames. On the set of 2017's *Lady Bird*, Saoirse Ronan coined "Pony" because he had a tendency to show his affection by nuzzling "and I think of him as a boy horse," the actress explained on *The Graham Norton Show*, as Timmy sat beside her red-faced. The costars reunited for 2019's *Little Women*, also featuring Florence Pugh, who years earlier let slip her secret name for Timmy when they first met at the 2017 British Academy Film Awards. "I accidentally called him Timothée Chalamala-Bing-Bong to his face," she recalled to the *Guardian*. The nickname became a Pugh family joke, and at the *Little Women* premiere, Florence's grandmother gushed to her, "I met Timothée Chalamala-Bing-Bong!"

TIMMY'S TOP TEN

A true cinephile, Timmy's passion for film goes far beyond acting. Storytelling, character development, and emotionally connecting with the audience has always captivated him—and continues to influence his approach to filmmaking. Just like his own catalog, his favorite flicks run the gamut of genres, from coming-of-age dramas and romantic comedies to big-budget blockbusters, and to esteemed directors he has gone on to work with himself, such as Christopher Nolan and Luca Guadagnino. These are ten of Timothée's all-time favorite movies and the significance of each, in his own words.

THE DARK KNIGHT (2008)

The sequel to *Batman Begins* and the second film in Christopher Nolan's trilogy, it introduces one of Gotham City's most notorious villains, The Joker, played to perfection by Heath Ledger. In fact, it was his performance that convinced twelve-year-old Timmy to take acting seriously—and it remains at the top of his all-time favorites. "For me, it accomplished all the amazing behavioral acting and storytelling that I loved, but also that big spectacle, shake-the-theater feel," he explained to IGV in 2023, fifteen years after first seeing the superhero flick starring Christian Bale, whom he shared the screen with in the 2017 Western *Hostiles*.

LA LA LAND (2016)

Timothée was a promising actor on the precipice of superstardom when he took an Uber from Midtown Manhattan out to Brooklyn to see Damien Chazelle's musical film about a jazz pianist (Ryan Gosling) and aspiring actress (Emma Stone) who fall in love while pursuing their dreams in Hollywood. "Watching *La La Land* was so inspiring," he said in an interview for YouTube channel *The Oral History of Hollywood*. Timothée, who was twenty at the time, brought along his grandmother, a former Broadway dancer, to see the Academy Award–winning film "and it felt like an ode to her life and cultural experience as an audience member of American art and the American Songbook."

AMERICAN PSYCHO (2000)

It's no secret that Timothée is a big fan of Christian Bale, and he's especially "crazy" about the English actor's unhinged portrayal of 1980s yuppie serial killer Patrick Bateman in *American Psycho*. In fact, he studied the satirical horror flick before an audition early in his career for the A&E series *Bates Motel*, the origin story of *Psycho*'s Norman Bates. "I went to Netflix, and the first thing that came up for "psycho" was *American Psycho*, which is obviously very specific tonally and performance-wise," Timothée recalled to *Backstage*. "So there's an audition for *Bates Motel* somewhere that's a Patrick Bateman impression that's *way* off tonally."

JAMES WHITE (2015)

Most people have probably never heard of Timothée's favorite film, but if you watch it, you will never forget it. Christopher Abbott stars as a twenty-something unemployed writer overwhelmed with caring for his terminally ill mother (Cynthia Nixon) in New York City. *James White*, which costars Timothée's friend rapper Kid Cudi is based on director Josh Mond's own experience. "It's a testament to the filmmaking that I couldn't tell where the filmmaking was," Timothée explained in *VMan* magazine in 2018. "It felt like watching a man's journey. Josh has his finger on what it is to be alive now."

BLUE VALENTINE (2010)

Timothée's favorite love story chronicles the beginning and end of a relationship, starring Ryan Gosling and Michelle Williams. "The acting's so good in that," he said of *Blue Valentine*, which is told in two linear narratives: when the couple first met and later during the dissolution of their marriage. To prepare for the latter timeline, Gosling and Williams lived together like husband and wife with their onscreen daughter in rural Pennsylvania, sharing one bathroom and grocery shopping on a weekly budget that reflected their characters' near-poverty. What resulted was the

"I don't know why it's not like everybody's favorite movie."

greatest performances of their careers thus far, and Williams earned a Best Actress nomination at the 2011 Academy Awards.

BIRDMAN (2014)

In a story that loosely resembles his own, *Batman* actor Michael Keaton stars as Hollywood has-been Riggan Thomson, best known for playing the superhero Birdman, as he attempts a comeback on Broadway. Timothée saw *Birdman* "six or seven times" in the theater and regularly rewatches his favorite scene: when Edward Norton's character, "the ultimate actor you never want to be," joins Riggan's production and immediately critiques his script. Years later, Timothée met Emma Stone, who played Riggan's daughter, and asked if she knew "how special it was" to be in *Birdman*, which won Best Picture at the 2015 Oscars. "It was incredible," Stone confirmed. "I can't even believe what [Keaton] pulled off in that movie."

BERNIE (2011)

While shooting *Interstellar* in 2013, teenage Timothée watched his costar Matthew McConaughey's acclaimed true-crime black comedy starring Jack Black as Bernie Tiede, a mortician who was convicted in 1997 of murdering a wealthy, mean-spirited widow (Shirley MacLaine) in small-town Carthage, Texas. "Jack Black is so incredible in that movie. I don't know why it's not like everybody's favorite movie," Timothée told film critic David Poland in 2017, admitting he had since seen the under-appreciated *Bernie* "like twelve times." The Richard Linklater masterpiece divided the citizens of Carthage yet influenced Tiede's early parole in 2014. However, two years later he was resentenced to ninety-nine years in prison.

PUNCH-DRUNK LOVE (2002)

Tied with Nolan for Timothée's favorite director is Paul Thomas Anderson, who gave Adam Sandler his first dramatic role: a lonely entrepreneur with social anxiety who is being extorted by a phone-sex operator. Based on the premise, Timothée assumed *Punch-Drunk Love* was a comedy. But it was clear in the first scene, as the character argues over a typo in a coupon promotion, "This was not a cheesy Adam Sandler comedy," he said in a 2018 speech crediting Anderson as an inspiration. "I sat there watching and watching and watching, and then something happened, it clicked. I was inside the world of an introvert . . . Adam Sandler clued me into a world I'd never been, and then it was over."

GOOD TIME (2017)

Twilight fans will see a different side of Robert Pattinson in the riveting crime drama about a small-time criminal who must spring his developmentally disabled little brother from Rikers Island (while avoiding arrest himself) after the two rob a bank. Timothée praised *Good Time*—which has a 91 percent approval rating on Rotten Tomatoes—as "a no-holds-barred thriller that provided shock and awe" in a 2019 *Variety* op-ed celebrating the film's directors, brothers Josh and Benny Safdie. But he saved the highest compliment for Pattinson, his costar in *The King*, describing his performance as "devastatingly seductive and deceptive."

I AM LOVE (2009)

Eight years before Luca Guadagnino changed Timothée's life forever with *Call Me by Your Name*, he directed *I Am Love*, about a wealthy, unfulfilled matriarch (Tilda Swinton) who has an affair with her son's friend, resulting in the destruction of her Italian family. One scene in particular grabbed Timothée's attention: when Swinton's character, Emma, is laying in nature with her lover. "That really jumps out at me," he said on Australia's SBS, "just the cool intimate closeness to the grass and the insects in the grass." *I Am Love* is the first installment of Guadagnino's *Desire* trilogy, which concluded with *Call Me by Your Name*.

WORDS OF WISDOM

When young Timothée arrived in Hollywood, some of the most famous actors on the planet took the time to give the newbie a piece of advice. The first was his *Interstellar* costar, Matthew McConaughey, who suggested he "take a little Timothée time" every once in a while as his fame continued to rise. "Because, you know, there's the acting side and then there's the celebrity side. The celebrity side turns the world into a bit of a mirror."

Leonardo DiCaprio, whose career most closely relates to Timothée's, kept it simple: "No hard drugs and no superhero movies," both of which he's followed, although he admits he's not adverse to donning a cape if it was the right project.

One of the most thoughtful gestures was from Tom Cruise, who sent Timothée "the most wonderfully inspiring email" after they met in 2019. The note included a list of stunt trainers for the *Dune* actor to contact. "He basically said, in Old Hollywood, you would be getting dance training and fight training, and nobody is going to hold you to that standard today. So, it's up to you. The email was really like a war cry."

ACKNOWLEDGMENTS

While writing this fan guide, I'm pretty sure I caught Chalamania—and I fear the only cure is even more Timothée! He's truly a national treasure, a rare talent with the most endearingly quirky personality, and I can't wait to see what he does next.

ABOUT THE AUTHOR

Kathleen Perricone is a biographer with published titles about Marilyn Monroe, John F. Kennedy, Anne Frank, Barack Obama, Taylor Swift, Beyoncé, and dozens more. Over the past two decades, Kathleen has also worked as a celebrity news editor in New York City as well as for Yahoo!, Ryan Seacrest Productions, and for a reality TV family who shall remain nameless. She lives in Los Angeles.

© 2025 by Quarto Publishing Group USA Inc.
Text © 2025 by Kathleen Perricone

First published in 2025 by Epic Ink, an imprint of The Quarto Group,
142 West 36th Street, 4th Floor, New York, NY 10018, USA
(212) 779-4972 www.Quarto.com

All rights reserved. No part of this book may be reproduced in any form without written permission of the copyright owners. All images included in this book are original works created by the artist credited on the copyright page, not generated by artificial intelligence, and have been reproduced with the knowledge and prior consent of the artist. The producer, publisher, and printer accept no responsibility for any infringement of copyright or otherwise arising from the contents of this publication. Every effort has been made to ensure that credits accurately comply with information supplied. We apologize for any inaccuracies that may have occurred and will resolve inaccurate or missing information in a subsequent reprinting of the book.

Epic Ink titles are also available at discount for retail, wholesale, promotional, and bulk purchase. For details, contact the Special Sales Manager by email at specialsales@quarto.com or by mail at The Quarto Group, Attn: Special Sales Manager, 100 Cummings Center Suite 265D, Beverly, MA 01915 USA.

10 9 8 7 6 5 4 3 2 1

ISBN: 978-0-7603-9690-2

Digital edition published in 2025
eISBN: 978-0-7603-9691-9

Library of Congress Cataloging-in-Publication Data

Names: Perricone, Kathleen, author. | Butcher Billy, illustrator.
Title: Timothée Chalamet is life : a superfan's guide to all things we
   love about Timothée Chalamet / written by Kathleen Perricone ; illustrated by
   Butcher Billy.
Description: New York, NY : Epic Ink, 2025. | Summary: "Timothée Chalamet
   Is Life is a beautifully illustrated guide that explores and celebrates
   the actor and his films"— Provided by publisher.
Identifiers: LCCN 2024049105 (print) | LCCN 2024049106 (ebook) | ISBN
   9780760396902 (hardcover) | ISBN 9780760396919 (ebook)
Subjects: LCSH: Chalamet, Timothée—Miscellanea. | Motion picture actors
   and actresses—United States—Biography.
Classification: LCC PN2287.C467 P47 2025 (print) | LCC PN2287.C467
   (ebook) | DDC 791.4302/8092 [B]--dc23/eng/20250102
LC record available at https://lccn.loc.gov/2024049105
LC ebook record available at https://lccn.loc.gov/2024049106

Group Publisher: Rage Kindelsperger
Editorial Director: Erin Canning
Creative Director: Laura Drew
Senior Acquiring Editor: Nicole James
Managing Editor: Cara Donaldson
Editor: Katelynn Abraham
Cover and Interior Design: Beth Middleworth
Book Layout: Danielle Smith-Boldt
Illustrations: Butcher Billy

Printed in China

This publication has not been prepared, approved, or licensed by the author, producer, or owner of any motion picture, television program, book, game, blog, or other work referred to herein. This is not an official or licensed publication. We recognize further that some words, models' names, and designations mentioned herein are the property of the trademark holder. We use them for identification purposes only.